All About MAN

Frank Gannon

LONGSTREET PRESS
Atlanta, Georgia

Published by LONGSTREET PRESS, INC.,
a subsidiary of Cox Newspapers,
a division of Cox Enterprises, Inc.
2140 Newmarket Parkway
Suite 118
Marietta, Georgia 30067

Printed in the United States of America

1st printing, 1993

Library of Congress Catalog Number 93-79662

ISBN: 1-56352-097-4

This book was printed by R.R. Donnelley & Sons, Harrisonburg, Virginia.

Jacket illustration by Mark Anderson
Jacket design by Laura McDonald
Book design and typesetting by Laura McDonald

ACKNOWLEDGEMENTS

I cannot deny myself the pleasure of seeming to look generous by mentioning people that helped me with this book. Laura Justin, Mandy Thomas, Jimmy Neal, Sara Entrekin, Tony Nickels, Sara Moon, Ann Clark, Heidi Mitchell, Shelley Rigo, Rocio Rodriguez, Larry Karp, and Clyde Melton. Thanks always to Paulette Piquet Gannon.

Much thanks to Mary Shue and her two guys named Dennis.

To Chuck and John, you are MEN, and thanks for it.

To Aimee and Anne, you've given me a lot more than I can ever repay. And lastly, Frankie Gannon, who will soon turn into a MAN. I was going to say that I couldn't wait, but that's not true. I can wait.

**FOR MY BROTHER BUD
FROM FORTY-NINTH STREET**

FOREWORD

MAN has been called the "paragon of animals." It has been said that MAN is "the master of all he surveys." Many have said that MAN was "made in God's own image." "What a piece of work is a MAN" Shakespeare wrote. Alexander Pope said, "The proper study of MAN is MAN."

That being said, let's have a look at this guy.

What follows is an exhaustive study of that thing we call MAN. I just wrote it, and I can tell you, I'm exhausted. My study took me all over the globe, figuratively speaking. Actually, I did travel over sixty miles, and I made some really long phone calls. I had to have several shirts cleaned, and I got into an argument with a guy at the post office.

It's been a long and winding road. I almost feel like Edward Gibbon who, when he finally finished *Decline and Fall of the Roman Empire*, wrote:

It was among the ruins of the capital that I first conceived the idea of a work which has amused and exercised near twenty years of my life, and which, however inadequate to my own wishes, I finally deliver to the curiosity and candour of the public.

Gosh darn it, that's pretty much how I feel.

Now when I was a young boy
At the age of five
My mother said I'm gonna be
The greatest MAN alive
But now I'm a MAN
I made twenty-one
I want you to believe me, honey
We'll have lots of fun
I'm a MAN
I spell "M"
I spell "A" child
"N"

That spell mannish boy
That spell mannish boy
I'm a MAN
I'm a full grown MAN
I'm a MAN
I'm a rollling stone
I'm a MAN
I'm a hootchie-cootchie MAN
Settin' on the outside
Just me and my mate
I made the move
Come up two hours late
Ain't that a MAN
I spell "M"
"A" chile
"N"
That
No
"O" chile
"Y"
That spell mannish boy
Don't tell me it doesn't
I slap your head with a brick

INTRODUCTION

Of all things of great importance, the subject of MAN is the least understood. For a long time, everything except MAN was being studied. We studied animals, but we seemed to ignore MAN, perhaps because of what we were afraid to find out about him.

We seemed hesitant to investigate MAN. Even now, we are really careful not to get MAN upset because we know that he would cause trouble. If we found out anything "sensitive," we were very reluctant to reveal it.

Some MEN say, "Hey, leave me alone. It's not your job to investigate me. Back off." I, for one, cannot accept this as a valid response. It is only by careful, scientific scrutiny of MAN that we may perhaps discover why MAN is here and what MAN should do. Perhaps we need to point out the direction that MAN should take in the future. Perhaps we may need to tell MAN to leave.

The present volume is principally an overview of my findings and suggestions based on my study of MAN. I know MAN isn't going to like some of what I say here. Some of it is painful reading, but then reading about MAN has got to be painful. It's got to be dogmatic and it's got to be tedious. It's got to be vague, and it's got to be indefensible.

It's got to be fair, yet it also has to be triple-checked against an inevitable slant towards frothiness and a celebratory air because the writer has found, after so many years of researching MAN, he's become prejudiced. With one or two exceptions, he just likes the hell out of MAN.

That's what I've tried to do.

AUTHOR'S NOTE:

This book you are holding is also available in another, more costly edition. That edition comes with a metal cover and is illustrated with photographs of me and my friends. Many of my friends, it occurred to me yesterday, happen to be lesbians with tattoos. I'm glad, however, that you chose to purchase this less costly edition. It shows that you understand a bargain when you see one, and your mother wouldn't like seeing that other edition on your coffee table when she comes to visit anyway. You're better off with this edition. You can look at the other one when you're at the library.

CONTENTS

All About MAN

MAN: His Origins

MANY, MANY YEARS AGO, BEFORE THERE WAS GEORGE Jessell, the earth was a simmering cauldron, an amalgam of the elements, the very stuff of existence itself, slowly cooling, much as today's jello molds do in the refrigerator.

There was a lot of hydrogen and oxygen and silicone (which would become important in the creation of breasts, as we will see later). There was latex and bondo and naugahyde, but one thing was conspicuous by its absence.

MAN.

There weren't even any animals. There was just a big, bubbly, slowly-cooling thing. And while it cooled, you could listen to Stravinsky's "The Rite of Spring." MAN didn't appear until much later—at least a half-hour after Mickey Mouse and the water that got out of control.

When MAN did finally arrive on the scene, he was naked, short, and a chain smoker. It took him a very long time before he learned to talk. At first he just made Brando-like mumbles. But then, just as suddenly as he had appeared, he started talking. He talked about all kinds of things, but his speech was dominated by one theme: I WANT SOMETHING TO EAT

AND SOME PANTS.

In time, he found both.

MAN first appeared in northern Africa. There he assembled with other MEN into "tribes." These early tribe MEN were very busy attempting to establish "culture." Their effort involved a lot of discussion and, ultimately, fist fights. Soon, ashtrays were invented, and civilization as we now know it, started to fester and coagulate.

The first MEN were little, short aggressive guys. Today their progeny live in north Jersey, but back then they were the emperors of the species. They pushed other primates, such as monkeys and gibbons, all over the place. They insisted that the "lesser apes" pay them protection money, and the lesser apes went along with it. They had no choice. By now, MAN controlled everything. A few gibbons got beat up in the weight room, and the rest of the apes caved in.

MAN was now in an extremely powerful position. At this time, MAN ran all of the continents and the water in between. If you even wanted to fly over MAN's "turf" you had to arrange some form of payment. Many birds resisted this. Finally the leader of the birds met with MAN in an attempt to form some sort of compromise. Some sort of compromise *was* met. MAN came out of the bathroom after dinner and shot the leader of the birds six times in the head.

MAN owned everything. The land. The seas. The air. The police.

The era of MAN had begun.

There is, of course, a big question. How did MAN, himself obviously a monkey, learn how to do all this stuff that obviously beat the living crap out of the other monkeys? Why didn't a well-prepared gibbon, for instance, discover electricity? Why didn't a baboon, who had crammed really hard and pulled all-nighters, figure out how to make a driver's-side air bag?

This is a big question. That's why we say that it's a big question. Some even call it THE big question.

But like most puzzling conundrums, this one seems to have

an easy answer. I don't know.

MAN was certainly no smarter than, say, a spider monkey. He was outweighed by the orangutan, and a gorilla would have probably beat him up really bad and just left him in a parking lot.

Yet MAN triumphed. He triumphed because I, for one, was behind him. I hated those other monkeys. I hated the way those baboons would just sit around with that smirk on their faces like they owned the place. And the lemurs, don't get me started on those assholes. They'd just hang there with those stupid eyes.

At least I respected the gorillas. If you had a problem, they would help you out. Sure, they were surly. That's just the way they are. But they'll help your ass out. That I will tell you.

I know—MAN can be sneaky, but he's a *lot* better than mandrills. You can keep those mandrills. Make a weekend guest out of a mandrill and then tell me about mandrills.

MAN is a shaper of his landscape. He is not, like the inferior "lower" animals, just a part of the landscape. MAN can build his own landscape, or paint it. MAN can paint his landscape, take it downtown, lean it up against a building, sit next to it, and try to sell it. Fat chance.

Every landscape in the world contains animals that have adapted to that landscape. (We're not talking about painted landscapes anymore. That was last paragraph. Pay attention.) In the eighteenth century, for instance, Indians used to talk about "dancing fish" that came out at high tide on the California coast. This is an extreme example of animal adaptation. These fish would dance to almost any kind of music, but that classic "big band" sound was what really turned them on. Late in the day, as the sun slowly disappeared into the Pacific, the Indians would gather and watch the dancing fish twirl and gyrate to the sounds of Benny Goodman and Kay Kaiser.

Every place in the world is filled with examples of animals that have adapted to their environment. MAN, however, as the "boss hawg" of animals, doesn't have to adapt. If he doesn't like his particular environment, he can change it. A hedgehog will just crawl under a bush, fall asleep, and wait for spring. If MAN wants spring, he can get spring. He can crank up the outside heaters and head for WalMart to buy any variety of plastic flower. Then he can watch video tapes of baseball games while he washes his car. MAN doesn't have to adapt. Adapting is for losers. Like hedgehogs. If, however, MAN happens to, for whatever reason, admire the hedgehog, MAN can adapt too. He too can crawl under a bush and wait for spring. But MAN doesn't *have* to. The hedgehog does. That's the key difference.

I once had a cousin who would, every year, come December 21, the first day of winter, crawl under a bush (making sure that there weren't any hedgehogs already there). MAN is free. If he wants to go the hedgehog route, that's an option that he has.

Biological evolution has, then, not shaped MAN into any specific form to fit into any specific environment. Compared to the sturdy hedgehog, for instance, MAN has hardly the equipment to survive on this planet. I, for instance, don't even have a good winter coat. Yet MAN not only survives, he prospers. This is because MAN, using his great intelligence and subtlety, doesn't really need any equipment. Indeed, MAN has turned his deficiencies into assets. For example, I have used my lack of a winter coat as an excuse to get out of shoveling snow. I have used the fact that I don't have shoes on as an inventive way of avoiding taking out the garbage. The history of MAN is filled with examples of MAN using his deficiencies to his advantage. This ingenuity is, along with his nice ears, one of the greatest of MAN's qualities.

MAN has changed a great deal over time. Today's MAN hardly looks like earlier MAN. MAN's thumbs are longer today. His head is larger. He's taller, and he has a better tan, although he's beginning to lose a little bit of his hair. That's why he's combing it funny, but one of the great ironies of MAN is just this: he's not fooling anybody.

We have found skulls that are two million years old. By

studying these skulls, we have come to two striking generalizations. Ancient MAN was called *Australopithecus*, and ancient MAN, primitive as he was, knew how to spell his name.

It is very odd to think that today's MAN came from these ancient origins, but he did. We know this because of exhaustive research and the fact that we saw it on PBS.

There are many animals that are sort of genetic cousins of MAN. The lemur is one of these. Just last week I remember feeling very guilty because I hadn't called my cousin Bill, a lemur, since last Christmas. I walked right over to the phone and started to look up his number when I remembered that the last time he was over, he ate part of my sofa. So I said screw it.

The biggest difference between MAN and the primates who preceded him was the size of his brain, which made complex behavior possible. While the size of the brain is not a true indicator of an organism's intelligence, it's a lot surer than going by the number of nostril hairs, a measure which early anthropologists, in a sad display of backwardness, used to employ.

Even a really big gorilla doesn't have that big a brain. Even King Kong was a relative "pea brain" when compared to the awesome grey matter that MAN packs. MAN's brain has been known to be as large as 2,000 cubic centimeters, which is really big, but I couldn't tell you exactly how big because I'm pretty confused about the whole metric thing, to tell you the truth. Suffice it to say that MAN's brain is plenty big enough to do the job. Nuff said.

MAN's brain was not only larger than everybody else's, it was very, very, very, complex. MAN was capable of taking twenty semester hours and pulling a three-five. However, there are no fossil remains to show us what the insides of his brain looked like. Modern MAN's brain is composed of grey, squishy-looking stuff, so we might surmise that primitive MAN's brain looked the same, but maybe with less squishy stuff.

With this brain, MAN did a lot. He made tools and weapons.

He went on hunts. Large groups of primitive MEN dressed in camouflage clothes and went out in the woods and killed animals and, occasionally, each other. The women usually stayed home tending to the fire and secretly ridiculing the MEN for their stupid macho posturing. But MAN didn't care. He would hunt antelopes and gazelles, and afterward, as the ancient sun disappeared into the ancient horizon it was what these ancient MEN called "Miller Time."

One of early MAN's first breakthroughs was the discovery of fire. MAN soon discovered that all of the other animals were afraid of fire, and this made MAN very smug. When that first MAN came out in his lab coat and told the other MEN about fire, there was much excitement. Unfortunately, we don't know who it was that came up with fire, so we can't thank him.

Soon after fire, of course, came cooking. No longer would MAN have to eat tartar after tartar, which must have been tedious and very hard on the teeth.

With cooking, however, came another problem. Tipping. But we will get into that matter later, after some coffee.

Where is MAN today? At what stage of development? Has he gotten better? Or has he gotten worse? When we look at MAN today, are we proud of him? Do we want to run up and give him a big hug and tell him that he's just the nicest, tallest thing?

I don't think so.

MAN today obviously needs work. Some need a kinder, more caring outlook. Some need a heightened appreciation of WOMAN, HIS FELLOW CREATURE ON THE PLANET WHOM HE HAS BEEN NEGLECTING LATELY. Some MEN you just want to run up to and slap. Others have bad posture and poor eating habits. MAN needs major work, and I'm afraid it's going to be expensive.

When I began life as a MAN, it was the fifties. Although I was very young and short I noticed the way that the older, taller MEN were. It was enough to make you sick.

In the fifties, MEN never cried. They were taught to suppress their emotions. This restraint was their only good quality. They were otherwise completely loathsome. They lacked compassion. When they saw a flatbed truck go by packed full of little screaming children, a fifties MAN would just start scratching himself and talk about football. Also, MAN in the fifties was dangerously unbalanced and actually thought of himself as male.

In the sixties, things got a little better—mainly because I was taller now and could influence MEN to be better. But still, try as I might, MAN kept acting poorly. In 1969 I told MAN that if he didn't stop acting like an asshole I was going to have to slap him. This aggressive posture worked for a while, but the improvement wasn't permanent.

Of course, then came the part of the sixties that most people are talking about when they say, "the sixties." As in, "I'm an accountant now, and you actually trust me with your money, but back in the sixties I used to like to eat a heck of a lot of LSD. And my hair was very long and looked stupid."

The sixties changed everything, and MAN was no exception. MEN questioned old values, rejected old truths, drove old cars. MAN was clearly becoming something new. And vibrant. And exciting. The Age of Aquarius was upon MAN, and MAN started to "do his own thing." MAN broke through old barriers and grew really ugly, thick sideburns.

This was a time of great transition. I, for instance, was barely three feet tall in 1960, but by 1969, I was big, mean, and bad, and was, for a time, the last white heavyweight champion. I had only recently gotten laid. Vast vistas stretched before me. It was really almost slightly better than average.

MAN in the sixties. Think of the names. Kennedy. King. Picasso. Ed.

In the sixties MAN was really one of the most "together" things that were happening. MAN could look forward and back. He could also turn sideways. Some could stand on their heads, and many could juggle.

I remember seeing a whole bunch of MEN. They were stardust. They were golden. They wore ridiculous clothes.

They were MAN in the sixties.

A long time ago, anthropologists thought that MAN was a relatively simple subject. Many anthropologists of that era considered MAN a "crip course."

"What are you taking this quarter, Bo?"

"Organic. Psych."

"What else?"

"I'm taking MAN. I gotta get my grades up or Dad's taking back the Mazda."

"Bummer."

Today, of course, we know that this is far from true. Today MAN is a real gut-buster, and only serious dweebs even think of signing up for it. Walk into today's MAN classroom. You won't see any Budmen in there.

In those ancient days, though, anthropologists thought MAN was a relatively simple matter. They called him HOMO ERECTUS ROBUSTUS. Since they were all MEN, it is not surprising that they gave themselves such a cool name. Today, though, we realize that they were way off. MAN is much more complicated than they thought, although he is, I grant you, quite robust.

It seems that there were really many more types of MAN than had been originally thought. There were dozens of them. They kept finding old skulls with different characteristics. They had to invent names for these MEN and somehow assimilate them into the big picture.

ROGET MAN

Between 1935 and 1936, in Biliton, a small island off the coast of Sumatra, in the Java Sea, a skull was found in a quarry. Robert Pikestaff of the University of London found the skull on July 13, 1935. Paul Wrensnest, a colleague of Pikestaff, confirmed that they had found the skull, but not in a quarry. Wrensnest insisted that they had found it in a pit. Pikestaff said that they had found it in a quarry, not a pit, but hc would find the term "open cut" acceptable. Wrensnest replied that he could never call it an open cut or a quarry, but he would find any of the following terms more than suitable: "vein," "load," "dike," "shoot," "lodestuff," "speed metal," or "esophagus." Pikestaff, at that point, turned to Wrensnest and told him to "fuck" himself.

ROBO MAN

In 1992, in Pennsauken, New Jersey, a partially decomposed MAN was found. He was far smaller than any previous species of MAN. Robo Man was less than half a meter in standing height. Yet he possessed an outstanding musculature. Also, astoundingly, Robo Man apparently had no dick.

CHEVALIER MAN

In 1950, in Cotes-Du-Nord, France, near the village of Dinan, in a deposit of the Second Interglacial period, a skull was discovered which sent an earthquake through the world of MAN studies. The portion of the skull that still retains its original structure shows clearly that this early MAN was completely incapable of pronouncing the letter "H." For instance, scientists theorize that he probably said things like "Tank eaven for lit tell girlz. Dey grow up in day most ay light full way."

In Chevalier MAN we see strong evidence that even very ancient MAN was capable of making you sick to your stomach.

RAGING MAN

He was found on the streets. Brooklyn. 1949. Once, before they got him to the lab for the autopsy, he asked the scientists to do him a little favor. The scientists said sure. So he asked them to hit him, as hard as they could, right in the mouth. Then he told the scientists that they punched like girls.

MAN and Society

THE SOCIAL PATTERNS THAT SHAPE MAN'S LIFE TODAY were first created in ancient camps on ancient beaches and midnight hunts in primitive forests. In sooty caves. In hooded glens. In rocky caverns. In dimly-lit supermarket parking lots. It was in these ancient and remote locales that the characteristic patterns of MAN's social life were first established.

First MAN had to move from his warm, tropical climate. He probably liked it there, but MAN is, above all else, an explorer. MAN must eternally go where no MAN has gone. He must go there, get diarrhea-like symptoms, and return, bitching and moaning on the way back. This urge to explore his world is perhaps MAN's greatest quality, the jewel in his crown.

When MAN moved, he met challenges—challenges that shaped him and actually formed him. Once you get out of the tropics, life gets tougher. There are seasonal variations in the food supply. Berries don't grow when it's snowing. And then there's snow itself. Early MAN had to learn how to shovel it, no mean feat. Also, consider something we take for granted—snowmen. Early MAN had to spend hours rolling big balls of snow to place one upon the other. Then there was the enormous problem: where to find a pipe and a hat?

We know, from very early cuneiform writing, that early MAN prevailed, despite these obstacles. Consider this fragment (circa 8000 B.C.): *In the meadow the tribesmen built a snowmen. They pretended it was Parson Brown.*

So now "Homo Erectus" (as his friends called him) had some new "stomping ground." All living things, from bacteria to tax lawyers, spread to areas of less concentrated population. In a million years from now, for instance, the Gobi Desert will be crawling with guys wearing double-breasted suits and wire rim glasses. That's just nature's way.

MAN moved east and west and north and south as far as he could, but he was finally stymied. When Early MAN got up around northern Canada, he probably said, "All bets are off, hoss. Too damn cold up here." When he first walked into the area that is today New Jersey, he undoubtedly said, "Man, it's dead around here."

So MAN isn't everywhere on this planet. He has done a pretty damn good job, though. A pretty goddamn good job of getting his little fingers in everything. One of the big aids that MAN developed in this area is this: MAN learned how to sweat, and he learned how to sweat, when necessary, like a pig.

MAN has a built-in cooling system and a built-in heating system. Plus, when it got *really* cold, MAN could always kill an animal and make himself a fur coat. He had to be careful, though. If the wrong people saw him, they would get very upset and start a long boring speech about "animal rights." The easiest thing to do, ancient MAN found, was to kill the animal and take its fur in secret. Then, when MAN ran into anyone looking at him suspiciously, he could say, "This? This is faux."

Another big change that came about as MAN started to spread out was pretty unexpected, but gratifying. A part of his body became much larger. Because this part was now so big, MAN just generally enjoyed himself a lot more and could hardly help smiling when he thought of how huge his "thing" was.

Unfortunately, I am referring to his brain. But with his larger brain came a lot of problems. Some of these older MEN, it now appears, developed *too* much brain. A skull fragment from Vertesszollos, Hungary, indicates that some of these ancient MEN were braniac-like beings of immense brain capacity. They found one ancient skull with a cranium capacity of over 1,400 cubic centimeters! That is huge! A guy with 1,400 cubic centimeters of grey matter today would be "boss hawg" in most any academic or scientific community. Today's average MAN packs much less brain matter—certainly at least a hundred or so fewer cubic centimeters. Today's MAN need not be concerned, though; studies have shown that a brain as small as 900 cubic centimeters can satisfy most women.

Why were these ancient MEN such chrome domes? Why did nature see fit to give them all that gray matter? On the surface it seems like a waste. Does a guy have to be a genius to forage through the woods and eats lichens and skin caribou? Probably not. It turns out that MAN developed that huge melon head because he was a rambling guy, always changing. All these changes made God say, *This species is going to need a big damn head.*

So MAN got one. His head today resembles a casaba melon. Big. Huge. Round.

However, MAN's tremendous brain gain did not come without a big price tag. It turns out that, as MAN's brain grew bigger, he turned more and more into a helpless little guy when he was born. Look at your average horse; it's up and around in a day or two. Consider cute little baby maggots. Before you know it they're adult flies, their adorable infancy now only a memory (unless you remembered to take pictures).

MAN, however, is just helpless when he is born. It's hard to believe that these tiny little babies ever get it together enough to drive trucks and bet on football. When MAN is born he is just about hopeless. The shocking statistics tell us that the average new-born MAN is unable to do a single push-up. Compared with most mammals, which come from the womb almost fully developed, ready to stand on their own, vote, and hold down at least a part-time job, MAN seems like a creature born before he is ready.

It is pretty appalling. Baboons, for instance, by the time they are a year old, have often gone off, married, *and* engaged in homosexual relationships. The human baby, in contrast, is completely dependent. He has to be carried. He has to be fed. Someone has to read him the newspaper. Someone has to drive; he can't. He can't even keep up his end in an argument, and, take him to dinner, guess what? You're paying.

Clearly, he's here too soon. He's too unformed to understand that you're not made of money. The reason he is obviously "born too soon" is interesting, so let me tell it to you.

During birth, a human MAN (in his baby stage) must come from the womb and pass through a bony opening in the mother's pelvis. If you recall, when you were a baby, your head was your biggest part. When MAN was first beginning to evolve into today's MAN, his brain and his head were increasing in size much faster than any other part of his body, or Mom's pelvis. So, if something drastic didn't happen, every MAN would have wound up with his head stuck in his mommy's pelvic bone, and that would have been the end of MAN as we know him. Conversation would have been difficult, MAN's words reduced to a low rumble from Mom's lower stomach.

But this didn't happen, thank God. What happened instead is that MAN's head does most of its growing when MAN is outside of mommy. When MAN is born, his head is only 25% of capacity. Our monkey friends have brains 75% grown when they're born. That's why monkeys don't seem to develop brainwise. A young monkey and a young MAN may be about equal in intelligence. Come back in a couple of years and MAN is consistently beating the monkey in most board games.

Because MAN is such a "slow learner," he has actually created society. Think about it. Society is just a whole bunch of people depending on each other, in much the same way that a baby depends on his mother: think about all of the people you are depending on right now—plumbers, doctors, mechanics, lingerie models. This interdependence is what human society is all about.

At one time, MAN had sex only at certain times of the year. Many MEN still follow this practice, but for today's MAN, it's a matter of choice. (I know that I plan to talk about MAN and sex in another chapter, but this discussion is not about sex *per se*. It's really about how MAN evolved as a social being. However, since MAN's sexual evolution is, as they say in traffic court, germane to the subject, I don't feel out of place in mentioning MAN's sexual evolution in connection with his evolving nature as a social animal. Also, I like to write this kind of stuff.)

The compelling factor in MAN's sexual evolution is the female of the species' estrus, or "heat." Today it is rare to talk about a woman being in heat, although I once saw an ad for the movie *Heat*, which read "BURT REYNOLDS IN *HEAT*." Today we usually speak of nonhumans when it comes to the subject of "being in heat." We say, then, that dogs "go into heat," although if I had known that humans at one time went into heat, I probably would have written a forged note like this in high school:

> Dear Teacher,
> Please excuse Frank from class yesterday. He was in heat.
> Thank you.
> Respectfully,
> Mrs. Gannon

At any rate, during evolution, this estrus cycle changed until human beings were capable of having sex anytime, anywhere, no holds barred. So today, no matter where he takes himself, he can look forward to big action regardless of the time of year. MAN as a species is quite fortunate to have developed in this manner. Let us imagine what things would be like under the old system. Hotels would be virtually empty until "heat week." Then they would be overbooked. Quite possibly, only young republicans would have the contacts to get a room.

Also, imagine the chaos and frenzy the "heat" system would cause on a personal basis. Under enormous time constraints, most would give up "choice of sex partner" as a viable option. Today, thank God, that's not the case. Men and women now get to choose when, where, and with whom they mate. Now human beings can choose sex partners and, based upon the quality of the sex, decide whether or not to form the partner-ships we now refer to as marriages.

But having choice also caused a problem. Early MAN lived in roving bands, and often these bands had more MEN than women, or vice versa, although even the bands with just one female were wise to make her the singer, particularly if she was attractive. Early bands that followed this practice got to play in many more bars. Another problem was that, since hunting was communal, food was shared. Therefore, one MAN was general-ly not responsible for feeding one particular woman. Neverthe-less, arrangements inevitably were made, relationships were formed. Certain women are going to like certain MEN, even if the MEN are wearing freshly killed animal skins.

There's going to be something about that MAN, that special MAN. The way he wears his hat. The way he sings off-key. The way he chews raw flesh. No, a primitive woman undoubtedly said, they can't take that away from me.

So, MAN and woman go travelling in this band. The MAN may not show it, but that he is probably thinking, "Bess, you is my woman now." Sure, they don't do that much together, except walk the plains and jungles searching for food and ani-mals to kill and eat. Relationships have been built on less.

In time, perhaps, this relationship starts to grow. They become closer. This guy is now walking next to that same prim-itive doll that he walked next to yesterday. They share private glances. They sit together and quietly share a laugh over that bison that crushed Ed's head on today's hunt. She leans over and whispers in his ear. He smiles. Such a funny world when you are young and in love and primitive.

Then, before you know it, the stork comes (along with the primitive couple, hopefully; see "MAN and Sex," a later chapter). So now there are little ones accompanying Mr. and Mrs. Primitive as they sojourn through the underbrush. Then, after a while, they are grandparents, valued for their wisdom, although they no longer kill wild animals that well. There you have it. The scene is set for human society.

All is not right with this picture. Even early MAN could tell that he was capable of evil, so he made certain tribal rules. No incest. No fratricide. No patricide. No matricide. No sorocide. No tongue on the first date.

Since you couldn't have sex with, or kill, anyone in your family, it logically follows that EARLY MAN went outside his immediate family for amusement. Soon he made friends by having sex with others from bands not his own. This practice is called "exogamy," the having of sex with those not related to you unless they're really good looking or you live in a trailer.

Soon MAN realized that his practice of travelling around in bands looking for food was not practical. Too many phone calls. MAN now built little "home base" places. Couples hung little paintings on the walls and put down carpeting. These ancient MEN asked their ancient women where the hell they wanted the chairs. This was a big step. Now MAN could go off for a few days, and when he returned the fires would still be burning and his women and children would be safe. Then the women would ask the MEN just where they had been for those two days, and the MEN would work on one of their most important inventions—lying.

These little bases were semi-mobile. If these guys were after wildebeests, or some other migrating animal, it probably became necessary to tear down the base and move. Over time, however, certain places became favorites, and early MEN returned to them perhaps seasonally. Unless they were headed to Las Vegas, an early favorite, they probably brought the family.

No other primate does anything like this. Most apes like to stay around one area their whole lives. Certain baboons have been observed to gather, 600 strong, on a cliff to spend the night. MEN never do this. Again, too many phone calls.

With a home, however seasonal, MAN now had certain advantages. He didn't have to abandon the sick or injured. He could let the woman, his fellow creature on the planet, stay home and make sure that nobody destroyed the place or sold them aluminum siding. He no longer was a traveling MAN, although some anthropologists argue that he probably had a pretty senorita from old Mexico who waited for his return, and a Stanford researcher has recently found evidence that he had a cute little Eskimo as well.

But the real importance of MAN's home was the opportunity for cultural advancement that it afforded him. Ancient MAN could gather around the fire and communicate. It was here that ideas, concepts, and miniseries were first allowed to fester and coagulate.

Although the home was a good idea, it did have its negative aspect. Once MAN *had* something, he developed a need to defend it. This quality is called territoriality. It is from this tendency, many theorize, that all violent behavior originates. All wars, not to mention the films of Macauley Culkin, support this hypothesis. If territoriality did not exist, there may have never been a world war, and, more importantly, there may have never been a *Home Alone Two*.

MAN and His Territory

MEN LIKE THEIR SPACE. EVERY MAN'S SPACE VARIES, but that particular MAN knows exactly where his space starts and your space ends. For some MEN, it's huge. Some MEN need an entire hotel lobby. With other MEN, as long as you're not actually breathing on them, it's okay.

This whole concept is related to the existential state that MAN finds himself in. He is, inherently, a vulnerable creature. He does not possess talons, for instance. With few exceptions (notably Richard Nixon), he does not possess a set of menacing, foreboding jowls. MAN has no spikes growing out of his head, except that occasional MAN who is later the subject of a *Ripley's Believe It or Not* cartoon.

Compared to, say, a stegosaurus, MAN is reasonably approachable. Even when he owes you money, it is often possible to walk right up to a MAN even when his eyes are set right on you. He can see you coming. Perhaps he will even stand motionless as you walk right into his space. Perhaps MAN will then go into some bullshit song and dance about how he doesn't really owe you the money—it's somebody else. Perhaps then you will tell him that you're really tired of the Brothers

Grimm, and maybe MAN should try Mother Goose instead.

At one time, this sort of behavior went unstudied. Today, luckily, researchers have pretty well explained it. The entire thing is genetic in origin. There is probably not a single, reputable scientist who believes otherwise. Territoriality is, science tells us, genetically determined. So you can let go of that guy. Let him up. His behavior is genetically determined. I said hurt him, not kill him. His behavior is genetically determined. You'll get your money.

Although we scientists now understand this concept completely, it does come as a shock just how recent our complete understanding has been. Until last Wednesday, for instance, many in the scientific fraternity thought that MAN was just being a jerk-off. Now, however, our great mother science tells us about Man and territorial nature, and we can all relax.

How can it be that numbers of MEN run around like Pac MEN and try desperately to keep other little Pac MEN out of their stupid territory? This is, again, another question for the ages, a question perhaps essential to MAN's very essence. Plato, in *The Dialogues*, was perhaps the first to address this issue:

MENON: Why are you always ragging everybody, Socrates? Put a sock in it. Even a whale comes up for air.

SOCRATES: Do you remember in the Elegaics?

MENON: What passage?

SOCRATES: Where it says: "A MAN who observes nature's words, who seeks always for the answer to the question, what does nature want me to do— that man, above all others, bites."

MENON: Bite this.

Why does MAN have this thing about space? If you look through books (other than this one) you will not find the answer. Most of them hardly treat the subject at all. *Peyton Place*, for instance, never even mentions it. *Flatten Your Stomach* completely overlooks it.

What are we teaching our children about this vital subject, the subject of why MAN gets in your face and you don't like it? Almost nothing. I have before me now some representative texts that are being taught to our children right now. Most of them just talk about the way MAN looks: his bones, his organs, his cells, and whatnot. None of these "learning tools" bothers to explore why MAN doesn't want another MAN peeing next to him if there are empty urinals. This is tragic.

Let's think about a subject whose behavior seems, on the surface, similar to MAN's, at least in his attitude toward his space. I am speaking, of course, of the common dog. Almost everyone has observed how the male dog characteristically wanders around, periodically pausing to pee on a certain spot before moving on. It is widely thought that the common dog (let's call him "Bowser") is "marking" his area. He is saying, in effect, "I am Bowser, I said. To no one there. But no one heard, not even a chair."

Now consider a MAN. Let's call him Neil Diamond. Certainly, he too goes from place to place, urinating as he goes. The parallels are so obvious, yet we choose to ignore or reject them, thinking, "Yes, that's it; I get it! But I can't draw parallels between MAN and a mere animal such as the common dog. That would be sick. My parents would hate me. I'm not going to do it. I'm not going to draw parallels between MAN and the common dog. I'm not offending Neil Diamond."

This anthropocentric attitude is so prevalent that often even scientists fail to perceive it. Yet it's always there, hovering around the edges like a border collie, nipping at our heels and forcing us back into the herd. The herd of big dumb people that are products of an educational system that is afraid to offend Neil Diamond.

That's why it was so refreshing for me to go to Europe and talk to people who have studied anthropology and written widely. People who neither know nor care who Neil Diamond is, although they do have some ABBA albums and enjoy listening to "Dancing Queen."

When I spent a summer at the Ecole d'tasty, a few miles outside of Paris, I witnessed, in a tightly controlled experiment, a couple of lemurs that shed considerable light on the subject. Lemurs are, of course, our distant cousins, and their behavior brought back to me a flood of emotions as I recalled the many incidents in my own experience that their actions evoked.

I remember staring at Claude, the larger of the two lemurs. Claude raised his striped tail straight up into the air. Then he walked over to me and grabbed me by my collar. He pulled me up until our faces were barely an inch apart. Then he gave me a little smile with his lemur snout.

"Why is he doing this?" I remember asking Dr. Leo D'Crock, the head of the institute, who was standing next to me.

"He doesn't—how you say?—like you," said Professor D'Crock.

"I'm not real fond of him," I said. "But I want you to do me a favor, D'Crock. I want you to lean over and tell this French monkey to get his hands off of me before I slap his little ass all over this laboratory."

D'Crock immediately leaned over and started whispering in fast French into the lemur's ear.

"Hurry up," I hissed. "I'm suddenly real anxious to pound me a little bit of French lemur."

D'Crock harshly whispered a few more words into the lemur's ear. The lemur gave me a hard look. Claude was a stocky lemur, about two foot six, with sloping, powerful shoulders and a scarred face that said that he had seen more than his share of lemur trouble. Our eyes met. There was a second where we just stared at each other without moving or blinking.

The tension in the air was palpable. It was thick enough to cut and enjoy with some French bread and a charming, understated dessert wine.

Then Claude put down his striped tail. He let go of my shirt and went over to the corner and sat down. Later that evening I ran into Claude at a bistro. He was with some gibbons. I bought him a drink and we talked about the war.

We never mentioned that afternoon again.

All right, we have noticed this behavior. Now, what do we do about it?

We theorize.

That's right. Despite the fact that research has been underfunded, despite the fact that MAN resists being put under a microscope (for the obvious reason), still, now is the time, ever so tentatively, to start talking about MAN's need for territory. Let's try not to get anybody upset, though. Okay?

What slight knowledge we do have in this area began in the 1920s. These "behaviorists," as they were called, tried to understand MAN as a big, complex, programmed machine. This approach actually started earlier, with Pavlov and his dog, later to be immortalized in the song, "Bitch," when Mick sang "I'm salivating like Pavlov's dog." This concept is, however, poorly understood, because after saying, "I'm salivating like Pavlov's dog," Jagger then sang the following: "Yeah wa ya nay me haw, my heart starts beatin' like a big bass drum. All right." Today scientists still puzzle over the ultimate meaning of Pavlov's dog. Is MAN reducible to a series of conditioned reflexes? Is the behavior of MAN ultimately understandable through a response-stimuli model? Can modern MAN, with a technology at his disposal far beyond anything Pavlov ever dreamed of, be on the verge of yeah wa ya nay me haw?

After Pavlov came J. B. Watson, an eccentric though brilliant researcher who was the first to explain the beginning of "Brown Sugar." ("Sho no fay about a fan a bye. Live ina market down in New Orleans.")

Today, Watson's work has been somewhat discredited after it

was found that he just looked at the lyric sheet. No fair, said science.

Nevertheless, during his day Watson's work shook the foundations of the MAN establishment. If he had listened to Donovan's records, he might have been immortal. Even so, many of his ideas have been assimilated into the mainstream, along with his body.

Pavlov's continuing influence illustrates that it was in Russia that the serious study of the grabby nature of MAN took hold. Today, however, many of the major scholars in this area are American, French, Danish, Lebanese, Galen, Coptic, Norwegian, and Himinbjorg.

In the 1950s a work exhaustive in its research appeared. This was, of course, *Dr. Spock's Guide to Child and Baby Care*. It was, however, a work that had nothing to do with our subject here. I just wanted to mention it because my parents never spanked me, and I believe that they were told not to in *Dr. Spock's Guide to Child and Baby Care*. I've always appreciated the tip, Dr. Spock. Mucho thanks and many more happy ones.

Today it seems clear that MAN is territorial. He doesn't have to learn this. It comes with the standard issue head. Just HOW territorial, however, is a learned behavior.

I learned, for instance, that if I stood too close to John Ferrucci in the lunch line, he was apt to turn around and slug me. I could, however, stand right on the back of John Bruni's shoes, and everything was still hunky-dory.

Let's go, once again, out into the field.

MAN and Sex

HIDING THE SALAMI
A Short Novel

By Arthur C. Clarke and Frank Gannon

The rain had not come for two million years. Here and there, in the tropical landscape, the earth appeared almost dry. The great fearful lizards had vanished long ago. Now hooved creatures thundered across the land in great herds. Here, near the middle of this planet later to be called Earth, in the continent that would later be called Africa, ape-men lived together in small tribes.

The ape-men hunted the hooved animals. But the ape-men were at war—at war with other ape-men, at war with themselves. Every day was another battle, and every day more ape-men died.

The ape-man was not well suited for survival. The hooved ones were swifter, more powerful. And the hooved ones did not kill other hooved ones. Only the ape-man killed his own kind.

The ape-men were always hungry. There was often a long time between the killings of a hooved one. Every day, when the first faint glow of dawn crept into the cave of the ape-man, the ape-man knew a gnawing hunger. The ape-man could not distinguish his existence from this gnawing feeling that was the great, great grandfather of all human emotion.

Ape-men came out of their caves with the dawn. WALKS FUNNY was an elder. CONFUSED LOOK was a young ape-man. They looked upward at the new dawn.

Then, from the dawn sky, it came. There was a huge, shrill sound. The other ape-men ran to the safety of their caves, but WALKS FUNNY and CONFUSED LOOK stayed. They covered their eyes before the blinding light. . . .

There was no more sound. There was no more blinding light. The two ape-men lowered their arms and looked at the object in front of them. It was long and blue and shiny. It had little fins in the back. In front there were two headlights. CONFUSED LOOK walked towards the thing. WALKS FUNNY watched.

The ape-man they called CONFUSED LOOK opened one of the doors. He paused for a moment, then sprang into the back seat.

The still tropical air was split by the sound of the ape-man's scream. The ape-man leaped and screamed and checked out the upholstery.

Visibility was zero. The altimeter registered 20,850 feet. Edwards waited. An hour. Two hours. Still no improvement. The weather was relentless. The snow fell wet and heavy. It had fallen for so long that it was hard to imagine the mountain three days ago when the snow had first begun.

Edwards and his partner Bronowski were not yet breathless. This was attributable to their long exercise sessions in the oxygen-deprived environment that their Chevies afforded them. Both had spent long hours in back seats going at it like racehorses. Nothing wrong with their bodies' oxygen retrieval systems.

The weather did not let up. Three hours passed without a trace of hope. Visibility remained virtually zero. Now, what had been unthinkable became a real possibility: not only might they fail in their attempt to scale K-13; now there was the very real possibility that they would never again get any pussy.

"Have you ever climbed downward in zero visibility?" asked Edwards. He was being very careful to use as few words as possible. He was only a few syllables away from having the hump machine turned off for good, and his words were clipped and harsh.

"Twice," said Bronowski. "Once in Washington State. Once in Africa. Both about five thousand feet. Nothing like this."

Edwards said nothing. A minute passed. Edwards put up his right hand, touching the mountain. A hundred splinters of ice rained down. He thought that what he was about to suggest was unthinkable, but he also thought that existence without getting any was equally unthinkable.

"Let's descend," he said.

Even from twenty million miles away, Jupiter was hard to ignore, its massive presence dominating the view from the R22 space capsule's window. Jupiter was a pale orange ball which seemed to float in the utter blackness of deep space. Its parallel bands, each wider than the earth, were clearly visible to the crew. Moving slowly through the cosmos, Anderson noticed that Europa and Io, Jupiter's massive moons, developed a sort of personality as he gazed at them intently through the telescope of the Biosphere Orbital Analytical Terminal (BOAT).

Although Europa and Io were many times the size of the Earth, Anderson felt a certain intimacy with them, as the space craft moved past them. Anderson's space capsule was travelling at many times the speed of sound, yet it felt to Commander Anderson that he was moving very slowly. Examining Europa. Feeling its roundness. Anderson wet his lips.

Then there was Io. Slightly smaller maybe, but quite delightful. So round and beautiful, and I am all alone, thought

Anderson. There was no one but Anderson, Europa and Io. Io. Especially Io. Now he could see how beautiful Io was, how soft her curves, how luscious.

Io and Europa were different, but that was what made it all so beautiful. Commander Anderson and the two beautiful moons of Jupiter.

Consider the possibilities.

Anderson did not dream, nor was he truly awake. He floated in a state somewhere between consciousness and dream. He felt himself being drawn inexorably into—what? A cave? A pool? A cloud? Concepts of solid, liquid, gas—all of these had transformed into something else, but what it was he could not give a name. He was far beyond naming. Perhaps he was far beyond what it is to be human.

Still he continued, deeper and deeper. He could no longer distinguish himself as a separate organism. He felt part of what was around him, but what was around him was utterly unknown to him.

He felt, slowly, almost imperceptibly, something start to invade his being. His instinct was to resist, yet he did not resist. What was this thing that was penetrating into his very essence? Like a thick fog moving in over a lake at night, whatever it was continued to permeate Robert Anderson, astronaut, age thirty-seven. Place of birth, Miami, Florida, United States of America, Planet Earth.

Anderson seemed to float in free space, while around him space stretched in its infinite blackness. He was utterly alone, yet he was not alone. He resisted and he welcomed. Once, in training school, a rope had snapped and he had fallen almost a hundred feet into a tarp set up for another experiment. As he fell, he thought that he was going to die. Yet he did not panic. He knew—or believed he knew—that all was well. He felt the same now. He abandoned himself to some greater power. It was a power that he was utterly ignorant of, yet he abandoned himself all the same.

As he hurtled through space, Anderson felt *himself* start to vanish. He did not resist. A strange sort of peace settled over him. He would be no more, Robert Anderson, astronaut, thirty-seven, Ph.D. University of Michigan, place of birth, Miami, Florida, United States of America, Planet Earth. This being would be no more, and in his place . . .

A dim feeling of consciousness appeared like a single intense spot at the core of his being. This spot spoke to him. Find yourself a Chevy, the voice said, then dust your broom.

Then he vanished.

EPILOGUE

There it floated, a glittering toy that no star-child could refuse, a 1957 Chevy with chrome mags and fuelie headers, dice on the mirror, and plenty of back seat.

He waited, marshalling his thoughts and brooding. For though he was master of the world, he was not sure of what to do next.

But he would think of something. He knew what he needed, that's for sure.

In the very depths of the cosmos, the star-child knew that it was time to play cosmic hide-the-salami.

The End

MAN is a sexual animal. If you see a MAN stalking through the underbrush, the chances are excellent that he is looking for sexual activity, although he may just have misplaced his car keys.

However, it's also true that, as far as sex goes, MAN has a lot of problems right from the start. All of MAN's basic sexuality is an inheritance from his days as a fruit-picking, forest-dwelling ape, but, as everyone who has tried it can tell you, it is very difficult to get a woman interested in fruit-picking. Also, the great majority of "today" women aren't going to move to the jungle. Most I've met get all huffy if you even mention it. So MAN is in big trouble and really confused. Just think of what MAN has to deal with as far as sex is concerned: he's a jungle guy who wants to talk fruit. No wonder there are so many sexual problems connected with MAN. It's a wonder any MAN ever "gets lucky."

Let's examine MAN and his sexual behavior. This is not as easy as it sounds because most MEN will get real testy if you walk up to them and tell them that you want to watch.

Also, MAN is a very complicated animal. If you say "sex" to a MAN, you can never be sure precisely what he's thinking. In MAN's relatively brief time on this planet, he's really gotten around. Even as I write the word *sex*, I recoil in horror at what must be going through the minds of you, the reader, if you are unlucky enough to be a MAN. God knows what kind of filth you're thinking. Do you kiss your mother with that mind of yours? I hope not.

Let's not narrow our discussion to the sexual practices of American MEN, which are, I grant you, appalling enough. Consider the whole wide world of disgust and mischief that MAN, the global animal, might get "into." (Pardon the expression. As a matter of fact, pretend that I have said "pardon the expression" every time I write something that makes your filthy little mind descend momentarily into gutterland.) There are over two and a half billion MEN on this planet right now. Some of these, I grant you, are rather young. Still, with those kinds of numbers, it's pretty safe to say that there's some really repulsive stuff going on right now, and if you see anything, please call the police or some nuns and get them to stop.

As unappetizing as it seems, some brave souls have actually gone to considerable trouble to study MAN and his sexual proclivities. They have discovered that sexual activity goes through certain phases. First there is pair-formation, which involves selecting somebody to have sex with. A MAN will usually choose a woman, but the partner can be another MAN, or, for the more adventurous, some species of woodland creature. We have all read about bestiality, which can be defined as sexual relations between a MAN and a "lower" animal. Once, in Confession, a priest asked me, after hearing that I had unfortunately had "sinful" (unmarried) sex, whether I had had this sex "with a woman, a man, or an animal." I felt like a provincial when I told him that it was only a woman, but I would try to improve in the future. Maybe next time I would be able to tell him that I had snared "the big three."

Pair-formation can be a very rough step. As a matter of fact, some MEN never get beyond this step. In high school, MEN often tease each other about their pairing-off difficulties. Later, MEN characteristically comment on it in a different manner. "You gettin' any strange pair-formation?" is a question often heard among older MEN who own trucks.

After pair-formation comes what these brave researchers call precopulatory activity. My hands shake when I merely write the words "precopulatory activity," so my hat's off to these researchers for actually studying it.

Precopulatory activity involves a great deal. There are complex facial expressions and ritualistic lip movements. This activity is followed by certain vocalizations, "oooh" being the most common. People engaged in precopulatory activity characteristically interact in a complex hierarchy of postural and auro-larynginal signals. They look at the clock frequently and raise their eyebrows and look at each other and mouth the expression, "Let's go." At that point they are drawn into a really boring discussion, and they try to be polite and figure out a way of communicating "We're leaving" without mentioning that they are leaving because they want to go engage in pre-copulatory activity.

After they get out of there (twenty minutes after that guy asked them whether they thought that Oliver Stone is *actually* a *mythologizer!*) it's time for what many consider to be the most pleasurable part of precopulatory activity.

First comes hand-to-hand contact. This isn't a good part, and the less said about this the better.

Then comes arm-to-arm contact, which, again, is not really one of my favorites. I've never had any memorable arm-to-arm contact while engaged in precopulatory activity, and I pray to God that you haven't either.

Then comes mouth-to-mouth contact, which is a much more fertile area for study. The question of the tongue has bedeviled researchers for centuries, and I guess it always will.

Then comes a period of running in slow motion along the ocean, usually accompanied by some really suck-o music. This part of the ritual may take as long as three minutes, so you might think about heading to the bathroom.

Then MAN and his companion walk out into an esplanade with a huge fountain in the middle. MAN takes out a coin, checks to make sure that it's less than a quarter, and throws it into the fountain. MAN turns and looks deep into the eyes of his pair-formation designated sex partner.

Since they're in Italy or someplace, MAN characteristically says, in a low voice, "Ronsoni so no buoni. Ronsoni is so good."

Then comes the part that I'm not quite sure you're prepared to hear about. We call this part copulation, and if there are any children reading this book they should stop right now because this is going to get really dirty.

The key word here at the beginning is *horizontal*. This phase may involve Days Inn, but I hope not for your sake. Certainly, getting horizontal on the side of the road is no worse. Plus, you don't have to worry whether the TV works when you're supine in the gravel by the side of the interstate.

Body-body contact comes next, starting out "low intensity" but swiftly proceeding to "high intensity." From there you proceed to "high-impact-Jane-Fonda-turbo-rotor-powered activity."

I must admit here that, as an Irish Catholic, I am scarcely able to do justice to this area of research. But I'll try to go on. I know you want to hear this.

MAN and his tawny-haired temptress lie next to each other, putting their hands all over their flesh, which is now naked. Man brings his hand up the smooth plane of his pair-formation designated tawny-haired sex partner. His tactile sensations and varying pressures are a source of amazement and amusement.

Suddenly it's time to get busy.

All bets are off now, and it's turning into something for the ages. MAN is thinking breasts and vagina, and maybe his designated tawny-haired sex partner is too, but he hopes not.

He hopes that her mind, and possibly her hands, are somewhere else. In case of a tie, he hopes that he gets the hands.

Now comes biting. Not hard biting, but biting just the same. Call it a kind of gentle nipping, maybe some licking, but licking characteristically followed by the MAN gazing at his partner and muttering that phrase made famous by the Campbell Soup kids, "Umm, umm, good." Not every member of the species uses this phrase, but it has always worked for me.

Next comes full-body exploration—often better than a childhood trip to Sea World. It's that much fun, and it just may be the real reason that MAN even bothers to stick around.

When you set out exploring, it's best to bring a map. Your scout master told you that a long time ago and it's still true. If you don't have a map, my first thought is, what's the problem? Are you too cheap? Are you waiting for them to start giving them out free at gas stations again?

If you are, as the Romans said, *sine* map, let me give you some general guidelines. I am, of course, assuming that you are a MAN. If you are a woman, however, please let me know how accurate the following map is. Let me leave two phone numbers:

(For regular women) 1-555-1212

(For the tawny-haired) 1-800-TAWNY

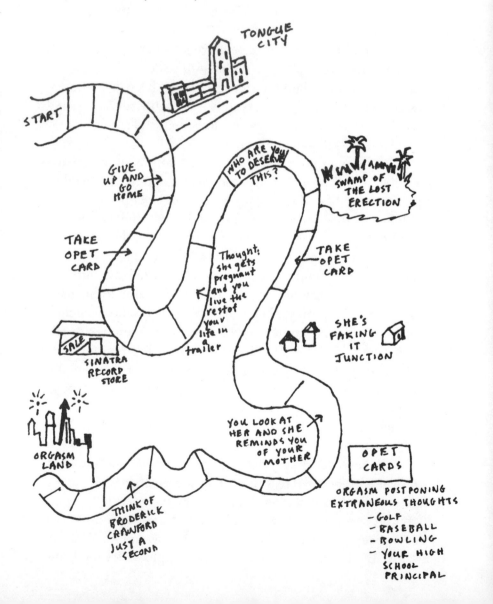

The orgasm, for MAN, is a violent, tension-releasing experience. Women are rumored to have a similar experience, but much more research is needed in this area. If you are a woman scientist interested in research, please get in touch with the author. The numbers again are:

(For scientists) 1-555-1212

(For tawny-haired scientists) 1-800-SCIENCE

At this point, we come (see earlier apology for phraseology) to one of the great paradoxes. Concerning orgasms, there has remained throughout history one undying question: why is it that a MAN will instantly have an orgasm if an attractive woman even looks at him, yet a woman often requires the lifespan of many vertebrates to do essentially the same thing? Why has God, a seemingly reasonable supreme power, designed things so poorly? Why is there this tremendous time gap between the two orgasms?

We'll examine the answer soon, but first I think we should try to form some kind of mental picture of how long this gap really is. In 1992, one researcher estimated that the total time between male and female orgasms was over a trillion years (if added together)! The mind can't really put that kind of number in perspective. Try this: a single white seagull flies to the ocean. He holds a small leaf in his bill. He flies out to the middle of the ocean. He dips the leaf into the ocean. He extracts it. It has a drop of water on it. He flies inland to Cleveland, Ohio. He shakes the drop from the leaf. He flies back to the middle of the ocean and repeats the procedure.

When that ocean is empty and the midwestern part of America is underwater, MAN is still watching television.

Naturally, this huge gap causes problems. Like most problems, however, this one has a solution. MAN has, through evolution, developed the ability, rare in mammals, to blame other people. In this case, MAN has decided that if women want to take several eons to reach orgasm, it's their fault—and their problem.

One unavoidable question remains. We know MAN. We know how slippery he is (see early apology). We know that something isn't right here. We know what MAN doesn't want to be known. We know that Man, while having sex with Miss A, isn't really even THINKING of Miss A. MAN's body is there (probably all sweaty by now), but his mind is somewhere else. And where that somewhere else is, is where MAN keeps Miss B.

The real truth is, MAN has Miss A, B, C, D and F. He's got a lot more than that, actually. He's got more Misses than Doctor Seuss has cats. They're crawling all over MAN's psyche. He's got them all over the place in there. Miss R might live in a trailer. Miss L might live under a desk. God knows where they all live.

At any rate, every MAN has a few favorite little places echoing in the canyons of his mind. Like Paul Theroux, MAN will visit these little places when it strikes his fancy. Unlike Thoreaux, however, MAN, when he visits, does not wear his pants.

I'd like to let you in on my own big secret. I would never be sharing this with you, the reader, if I didn't know that I don't have long to live. If I didn't know that I don't have long to live, then I would never tell anybody what I am about to tell you.

I am about to tell nothing less than what I think about when I "do it."

Bond reached for a towel and, wrapping it around his waist, lighted a cigarette and watched Miss Goodnight walk into the room and begin removing her clothes. He watched her quietly remove her plaid skirt and toss it on a chair. She stared at Bond with an attitude of wanton expectation. Bond reached over to the night table and took out a cork-tipped Turkish cigarette. Bond had previously smoked Players, and before that he had smoked ones that he found already partially smoked. It was something that he had picked up at Eton, smoking cigarettes partially smoked by other people.

"I've missed you, James," said Mary Goodnight. She was in her bra and panties now. Bond looked at her and she looked back at Bond who continued to smoke.

"I've missed you, too, Moneypenny," Bond said. Bond was tiger-muscled and she looked at him. She liked it. She liked the way that white scar ran down his tiger-muscled body. Bond was tiger-muscled.

"How much?" said Miss Moneypenny reaching behind her and unlocking her bra and letting it flutter to the ground and then sliding down her panties and standing there naked and looking at Bond with a smoky look in her eyes.

"Pretty much," said Bond. "Guess."

She moved closer to him. Their mouths almost touched. Bond put out the cigarette. He had a black comma of hair on his forehead. She tried not to think of that. Bond lit a cork-tip cigarette.

"This much," she said. She smiled and spread her hands approximately six inches apart.

"Pretty close," said Bond. His eyes were fiery and he was as taut as he had been the last time he had done twenty slow press-ups.

"When do we get started?" she said.

"Pretty soon," said Bond.

"What does that mean?" She turned and pressed herself against James Bond.

Bond took a deep breath.

"Now," he said.

His mouth came ruthlessly down on hers.

The undisputed king of statistics, as far as MAN is concerned, is Wilt Chamberlain. He was, of course, a basketball player. Many say that he was the best ever. One thing is for sure: he has the statistics. People think that Michael Jordan is a great scorer because he averages about thirty points a game; Wilt averaged over fifty points a game for a whole season. There are sports-page headlines when somebody gets thirty rebounds in a game; Wilt got *fifty-five* rebounds in a game.

Lots of amazing numbers, but the most amazing number that Wilt came up with is the following:

> There are a few of us who are fortunate enough to be in a position to fulfill our lustful desires. I'm one of those lucky ones. So don't be shocked to hear that if I had to count my sexual encounters, I would be closing in on twenty thousand women. Yes, that's correct, twenty thousand different ladies.

Does he have a scrap book?

For the average MAN, the number is far lower. Although almost all MEN manage to have sex with over a thousand women, you, the MAN reader, do not have to feel inadequate if you've only had sex with seven or eight hundred. Perhaps you are still young. Perhaps there was some medical problem. The key thing to remember is this: it's not a contest! If you only have sex with, say, 810 women, that's okay. It doesn't make you any less of a MAN.

MAN and His Mythology

FROM HIS VERY EARLY DAYS, MAN HAS ALWAYS HAD myths. The word *myth* is a part of MAN's everyday language. Every schoolchild is familiar with that mythical figure, Santa Claus. Our myths are all around us: that "Mercury" guy outside of the florist; the giant rabbit who delivers eggs, the symbol of fertility, to our children; that doctor who doesn't care about money and is actually working because he wants to alleviate suffering; the MAN riding a zebra who throws women's panties on your lawn every February. All of these, though not real, are quite familiar to us, so familiar that they seem, in a way, more "real" than the world we actually see around us.

So MAN needs myths. Originally, they probably explained things to man. Ancient MAN saw a big flaming thing go across the sky every day, and his pathetic ancient mind was probably comforted in thinking, "That thing in the sky? That big yellow thing? That's Apollo in his chariot. Every day he drives it across the sky. When he leaves, it's night time. That's what I believe. It gives me comfort. You don't like it? You got a problem with that?"

Even today, when we know that that's not some guy in a

chariot up there (give me a break, what do I look like?), even today, modern MAN, for all of his staggering accomplishments, still needs myths. Today, modern MAN may look at the ancient myths from a different perspective, but the myths themselves still speak to MAN's deepest fears and desires.

Why can't MAN live forever? If he trains and eats sensibly, why can't he continue to exist until the end of time? This bothers MAN. It bothers the crap out of him. I'm having a good time, MAN thinks, why can't I continue to have a good time? Just when it gets good, some idiot has to pull the plug. Why? Why?

The answer to this question has evaded MAN since MAN started looking for it. Cagey bastard that he is, however, MAN has actually found the answer and written it in code.

One of the oldest myths on this subject comes from ancient Corsican fragments. It explains MAN's peculiar fate.

Our first ancestors were named Edna and Jerome. Jerome was a barbarian, but Edna came from the sky. When Edna's father found out that Edna wanted to marry Jerome, he stole Jerome's magic calf and took it with him back to the sky. Jerome went to the sky to prove himself worthy and get his magic calf back. He did this by completing a series of difficult tasks, like touching his nose with his tongue and brushing his teeth in the mirror. Jerome was given back his magic calf and allowed to marry Edna. They returned to earth, but as soon as they got there Jerome walked out back and died. This is how "death" started. Now go away.

The simple eloquence of this ancient tale still speaks to the deepest part of me, and probably you.

Today we think of science as "real." We think of science as "verifiable" or "true," yet science is just as mythological as mythology itself is. That's why conversations like the following, though commonplace, are so regrettable:

"Well, Bob, this looks like a rough quarter. I'm taking Calculus II, Organic Chemistry, and Advanced Genetics. What are you taking?

"I'm taking Mythology."

"Get away, you scab."

Take "the black hole" thing, or "the big bang" idea. Scientists call things like these "theories," but those in the know dismiss them as the mumbo-jumbo they are. If you happen to be one of those who "buy" science, good luck. You're going to need it. Give my regards to the tooth fairy when you run into him.

Because, Mister Smart Guy, science doesn't really tell you anything. It just offers theories and you buy them or you don't. Sure science is useful. Science helps us make dinner and watch television and relieve our indigestion, but it's not going to tell you what you're doing here. When science tries to tell you what you're doing here, it turns into mythology. Thus the famous explanation of Einstein's, "The most beautiful thing we can experience is the mysterious," and later, "Something deeply hidden had to be behind things," and later still, "Sock it to me."

And later still, "Who do you have to have sex with to get a drink around here?"

Perhaps by doing a little comparative mythology, we might discover certain strange parallels between these ancient stories, parallels all the more alarming because of the absolute separation of the cultures that produced the myths. Why, we might ask, does one culture, say Australian, have a creation myth that exactly mirrors the creation myth of a culture, say New Jersey, that is so remote from its own? Why are there these odd parallels between the mythologies of people who had absolutely no chance of ever seeing each other? What is going on here? Is mythology the language of God talking to MAN? Is there some sort of collective unconscious that we all share, much the way birds and other animals share certain instinctual knowledge? Is mythology telling us something almost unfathomable about our truest nature?

Personally, I doubt it.

Consider the myth of the deluge or flood. Almost every culture has its version of this ancient "occurrence," but did it really occur? It is impossible at the moment for science to tell us with any degree of certainty whether or not there really was a flood. Nevertheless, mythology seekers have compiled sixty-three versions of the flood story. These versions differ in details (in some, no water is mentioned, for example, and in another the deluge turns out to be a trick pulled by some kids). But the basic story is the same: it rained.

Perhaps the deluge story is metaphorical. Perhaps these ancient stories are merely symbolic. The deluge story, for instance, might stand for the state of human beings on the planet: it is always raining and they are always bitching and moaning about it. Yet they endure. Sorry, I didn't mean to say that. They don't just endure. They conquer. They prevail. Even though it rains, these ancient stories might be telling us, there's no reason to get all mopey. Look at Kathie Lee Gifford. Surely she is what our ancient ancestors had in mind when they told their deluge stories. It rains and many die. But not all die. And those that do not die are perky.

How then, is myth to be defined? In general, a community's myths are the stories that are traditional to its people; the stories that the older people tell the younger people. These are stories that have developed over long periods of time and through many retellings. It may be said that they convey the collective wisdom of many generations.

Here are a few myths peculiar to contemporary American culture. No doubt you're familiar with them.

- If you wash your car, it will rain.
- A watched pot never boils.
- If you are tall and wearing a suit, if you tell someone to do something, no matter how stupid, that person will do it. Provided you pay him what he usually gets.
- Take lessons, you'll do better.

MAN and Language

WHEN DID MAN LEARN TO SPEAK? AT ABOUT TWO YEARS old? Don't be stupid. I'm talking about MAN as a species.

Investigators have been looking into this question for a long time. Thousands of years ago, the pharaoh Psammetichus decided to experiment in this area. He got two new-born babies. He isolated them so that they could never hear anybody speaking around them. The pharaoh thought that he would find out what language human beings first spoke. This kind of experiment would probably receive federal funding today.

Centuries later, James the Fourth of Scotland tried a similar approach and reported that the babies started speaking Hebrew. The babies later got King James to invest in several businesses. Many theologians of that time accepted James's experiment because they felt that Adam and Eve probably spoke Hebrew, so it was quite reasonable that two babies, completely isolated from other languages, would independently learn and start speaking the Hebrew language. This story shows why many people continue to believe that dogs in spaceships landed on earth thousands of years ago, built pyramids, peed on them, and left.

Actually, to this point it's impossible to say precisely when MAN started speaking. He's been here a million years, and during that time period, he's obviously been running his mouth. Until the present volume, however, no one has been able to establish just precisely when MAN started making the sounds that we call language. Now, I am ready to come up with a figure, based on exhaustive research. (However, the figure, tragically, doesn't have anything to do with this subject.) Here's the figure.

MAN is the talking animal ("MAN, the talking animal: from Kenner!" will be big next Christmas, along with "MAN, the action figure" sold separately). As a talking animal, MAN has developed an enormously complex method of communication. If MAN touches his hat and rubs his belly, for instance, it means "hit and run." MAN is also able to use words to communicate, but words have never proven to be MAN's strong suit. MAN spends a great deal of time scratching his head and asking, "Could you spell that?"

MAN's language of choice is English. Although Chinese is spoken by the greatest number of MEN, English is obviously going to take off in popularity. English's popularity comes from its mellifluous sound, its vast vocabulary, and the fact that many English-speaking MEN have had really bad experiences learning French in high school and have gotten quite touchy about the subject and get very tense when they see foreign writing on menus and subpoenas.

So rather than feel stupid, English-speaking MAN has cleverly avoided learning any other language. Now smart-alec foreigners are forced to speak the Big Guy's language, and if they don't like it, they can just go back to cheese land.

Because English-speaking MAN is such a bad sport, we have funny looking directions written on many of his products. Everyone has encountered directions written by non-English-speaking directions writers. Almost every day, you see something like—

OBTAIN A SCREWDRIVER AND RESOLVE TO TITILLATE BOLT A WITH A TURNING OF COUNTER CLOCKNESS UNTIL QUIESCENCE IS ACHIEVED. THEN CAUSE TO BE DUPLICATURE MORATORIUM UNTIL A SMILE IS ON YOUR FACE BECAUSE YOUR INTERSTICE WITHOUT A PLEASURABLE UNIT SUCH AS THIS HAS SUDDENLY MADE A BEELINE AND YOU CAN SAY THAT YOU HAVE BEEN RUPTURED.

This situation is understandable because English is a very complicated language. It has been adopted by the world only because of the reasons stated earlier and a lot of payola. Consider a few simple examples of the strangeness of English. When I say, "I could care less," what do I mean? Don't I mean exactly the opposite of what the words say? How about when you look out the window and say, "It's raining cats and dogs"? Have you ever considered just how strange a thing that is to say? Or how about when you say, "I think I'm going downtown and fire my rifle into a crowd"? Odd language.

Consider just how many words there are in English. The Oxford English Dictionary lists over 600,000, and MAN actually uses about 200,000 of them on a regular basis. Also, many of the words mean the same thing as another word. Big and Huge. Vast and immense. Large and vast. Penis and dick. Moron and Quayle.

But one terrific thing about MAN's favorite language is its flexibility. English-speaking MAN can say "Shitfire, I just slammed the door on my goddamn hand!" *and* "Shitfire, the door was slammed by me on my goddamn hand!" This is a construction that is impossible in many languages. In these pathetic non-English languages, speakers don't even have a passive voice, and even if they did have a passive voice, they'd probably never use it without asking the U.N. if it was all right.

English-speaking MAN can also be emphatic, something he's very good at. This involves that all-important word *do*. As in I DO DECLARE. I DO GO AROUND LOOKING FOR SOME ACTION. I DO LEAVE SKID MARKS ON YOUR DOG, YOU PATHETIC EURO-TRASH WUSS WITHOUT THE EMPHATIC VOICE IN YOUR LANGUAGE.

English-speaking MAN, unlike his Wilma-like cousins across the pond, can also make his words serve several purposes. So he's got a noun, is he satisfied with a noun? No. He's got a noun and now he's making it into a verb. Consider the English word *head*.

(NOUN) I've seen better *heads* on boils, you euro-trash newt.

(VERB) Let's *head* over to where the non-English speakers hang and give them melvins.

English is a sleek, versatile, emphatic instrument. If you see a bunch of English-speaking MEN coming towards you, you better get ready to talk hard English or go join the pooh-heads across the pond.

English is also free of gender. This does not mean that regular MEN shouldn't talk it because neighbors will call them eunuchs behind their backs. What this does mean is you don't have to worry about whether a stapler is a boy or a girl, as unfortunate German-speaking MEN must. In English, a stapler is neuter, and that's the way God intended it to be, although I do have a letter opener that I consider pretty butch and address in the masculine.

In college I had a pillow that I called "Sally," but the less said about that the better.

So English looks like the choice of a new generation. But where did it come from? It seems doubtful that neolithic MAN called a rock *rock*, a cave *cave*, a tv remote control a *couch commander*. He probably used other words.

Nobody knows for sure just how old MAN's favorite language is. There probably wasn't anything you would call any language before 30,000 years ago. That's when we got the cave paintings at Lascaux, sophisticated tools, and the opening of *The Fantasticks*. None of this could have happened without anybody talking to anybody else.

Thirty thousand years ago MAN must have had a language complicated enough to express concepts like "There's a big bison-type creature over there. Let's attack him with this stapler." But English, the "total babe" of languages, was still a long way off.

Don't get me wrong. English is plenty old. MAN has been on this planet talking for at least twenty thousand years. Some of that time was spent "talking trash," unfortunately. Nevertheless, it seems a pretty good bet that when MAN wasn't talking trash about me and my woman, he was talking English.

The first speakers of English were the Anglo-Saxons. These were white people who never had sex but did eventually start playing golf and drinking way too much. Their MEN were characteristically ruddy-faced when they got older. The women members of this ancient people had shiny foreheads. They spoke through their noses, both sexes: What they spoke was English.

This was technically "Old English," but for my money it was good enough. If we went back to Old English, maybe some of these kids would start having respect for the older people who were here before them and stop bothering them for money every other weekend. Maybe if younger Americans looked at Stonehenge once in a while and thought about what THAT meant, we wouldn't be having all these problems with drugs and sexual intercourse and whatnot.

Today, mention Old English in public and you get nothing but a big cold stare. Nobody wants to hear about Old English. You never hear, "Bob, tell everybody about Beowulf again." You never hear it, and it's a damn shame that you don't.

What do we mean when we say, "Old English"? We mean

English as it was spoken before the Norman Invasion, which occurred when a whole bunch of guys named Norman suddenly showed up, and talked their way into sticking around for dinner. (Pretend I didn't say that.) To a modern English-speaker, Old English sounds like a foreign language, although a few Old English words have survived into today's English. As you might expect, these are among the most commonly used words in English: father, mother, brother, water, I.O.U., money, forgot, punch, mouth. Scumbag, also.

The early English speakers were actually illiterate in the sense that they could only speak their language, not read or write it. (They had a runic alphabet which they scratched on ceremonial furniture, thereby "ruining" it or "rune-ing" it. That is where we get our word *labioplasty*.) In 1985 a coin was found which has as its inscription the first "written" English sentence. No one has ever figured out what it says, but the coin is interesting in that it also contains the image of Abraham Lincoln smoking a cigarette.

The Anglo-Saxons were not only uncultured and illiterate. They were also pagan. They worshipped strange gods, practiced human sacrifice, and *never* said either "please" or "thank you." It is little wonder that this era is frequently called the Dark Ages.

Nevertheless, the English language comes from these people. Even though the people might have been pretty barbaric, their language has proved quite remarkable in its breadth of expression. Consider the vast variety of things written in this language: The King James Bible, *Hamlet, An Essay on Understanding, Lesbian Bikers on Holiday*. This ancient language of these primitive people has proved "up to snuff."

Then, of course, came the Normans, and with them, their invasion. There was a massive slaughter at the battle of Hastings, and now Normans were the rulers. For a while there the only people who spoke English were waiters.

Who were these Normans? They were really Vikings who happened to delight in the quaint and beautiful countryside of northwest France, and consequently slaughtered its inhabitants and took over. They spoke Norman French, a language very much like French except for the preponderance of the name "Norman."

NORMAN: Elle est aussi grasse que vous, cette viande, Norman.

NORMAN: Cretin!

NORMAN: Tata de luxe!

NORMAN: GO AWAY, NORMAN, YOU MAKE ME, HOW YOU SAY? SICK!

Yet, English, rather than French, became the dominant language. The regular people, the serfs, the peasants, the used-car salesmen, still spoke English. It probably didn't seem that weird to them that there were people speaking another language who seemed to be in charge. Lots of English monarchs before then spoke other languages, although some of them just frowned and pointed.

So, English won, although we still have a great deal of French words in our language. Consider *jury*, *felony*, *traitor*, *frog*, *shoot*, *cheese-eater*, all of which we owe to our friends across the pond.

Nevertheless, for three hundred years the English language had no official status. There were no rules. Roving bands of renegade speakers of English roamed the countryside speaking incorrect English. Believing themselves "born to be wild," these early outlaw English speakers thought nothing of making the verb not agree with the subject, dangling modifiers, splitting participles and killing nuns.

These were wild, untamed days for the English language. What written fragments remain from this era are virtually unreadable because of all the corrections.

THOU ART A WEASEL AND A KNAVE VARLET WHAT THOU HAST DONE TO MY SISTER I HATH HEARD AND I AM NOT THRILLED SO I THINK THAT I AM GOING TO HAVE TO DO THE SAME THING TO YOU BUD.

Underneath this fragment (c. 1288 a.d.) there is, written in another hand, this:

Thou shows good development of ideas, but your paper is very weak technically. C minus.

So English was allowed to run wild (often without being corrected or graded). Consequently, it was allowed to change, to evolve, and as it changed, it became simpler. Soon, it was virtually "uninflected." Any slob could learn it. There was no "agricola" business. No memorization, and quizzes were rare.

By the thirteenth century, English children were no longer expected to learn French before they went off to school. English was now dominant. French was doomed. The English speakers took over and started talking fast, hard English. No more pursing the lips, talking through the nose, drinking wine with lunch, smoking cigarettes, and liking Jerry Lewis. The French language was dead in England. Too bad. A real shame.

The French back home in France actually started to think that the Norman French speakers back in England sounded funny. Because English people actually pronounce words instead of calling every word OOOOOV, no matter how long it is, these pathetic ancient French people actually began to think of the English as "amusing" or "backward."

This is when Henry V went over to France and slapped their pursed, cheese-eating faces once and for all. Then he took back the king's daughter, married her, and turned her into a decent, English-speaking person who found it rather amusing that French intellectuals think Jerry Lewis is Shakespeare.

Now we had what is called Middle English. In the fourteenth century in England, what we call English was spoken by only some of the English people. They spoke in dialects so thick and varied, that a MAN from the extreme West would never be able to understand the MEN who lived only sixty miles to the East. Consider this imaginary conversation which clearly illustrates this point.

William: Do you like my oxen?

Harold: What?

The language that today is English comes from the way MEN who lived around the city of London talked. There were more MEN in London than anywhere else in England, so it's not surprising. Also, London English had certain appealing qualities. Almost all MEN, at one time or another, want to sound like James Mason or Rex Harrison or Johnny Rotten or Sid Vicious.

This was the period when English changed the most rapidly, the period that produced *The Canterbury Tales*, that book that you were forced to read. Did you really read it? Cliff Notes? Just the dirty stuff? Which is it? If you didn't read it, but you said you did, I suggest that you stop reading right now and call the person you lied to about *The Canterbury Tales*.

Don't you feel better now? With that weight off your back?

Even if you did read it, you probably read a translation because Chaucer wrote in a way that almost resembles a foreign language. Consider "Whan that Aprill with his shoures soote/The droghte of March hath perced to the roote/And bathed every veyne in swich licour/Of which vertu engendred is the flour." Does that sound at all like modern English? Indeed, it appears on first glance to be a foreign language. However, once you discover that the first line is, in modern English, "There was a young lady from Nance,/Who got on a train by chance," the "riddle" becomes clear. It's English.

Chaucer died in 1400, but as soon as 1450, a mere fifty

years after his death, a writer wrote the following, in this precise way:

> What's eight miles long and has an IQ of forty?
> The Saint Patrick's Day Parade.

Clearly, modern English had arrived.

Today, no matter where you go, you run into MAN's favorite language. In Taiwan, you can eat at a place called Joe's Bar and Grill. In Yugoslavia, you can get your pants pressed at Bob's Tailors and Drycleaning. In Paraguay, walk into any cafeteria and say, "Michelle! Todd!" and everyone will turn around.

So how many people in the world speak English. That's very hard to say. (Do you count Tom Brokaw, for instance?) Suffice it to say, it's a lot.

Despite the fact that English is so global, if you go to a country like Belgium, where almost everyone speaks English, you don't see many TV shows in English. Even if virtually all of the viewing audience understands English, the overwhelming majority of the people prefer to watch an American television show dubbed into their own language. This is because it's very amusing to watch, say, Hoss Cartright doing his Maurice Chevalier impression. The entertainment value here is quite clear, so you really can't blame these foreigners.

There are, of course, still many many languages being spoken in the world. I think, to obviate the trouble and expense of translation, it might be a good idea if everyone in the world learned a common language. They tried this before, if you recall. The proposed "common language" was called Esperanto. Do you know it? Me neither. Do you know English? Me too. Let's make English the official language of the planet Earth.

Nuff said.

MAN and His Obsessions

IRONICALLY, I HAVE FOUND THAT MAN, A LIVING BEING, can't really be adequately described without referring to MAN's life. In fact, despite my Homeric detachment, I find that I can't really avoid referring to my own life as a man. *My Life as a Man* was, of course, a novel by Phillip Roth—a novel wherein Roth, who was a great writer before and after *My Life as a Man*, wrote one of the real contenders for WORST NOVEL WRITTEN BY A GREAT NOVELIST.

I know that you don't want to hear about my real life. I can't think of anything worse than my life to write about, except, of course, Phillip Roth's life. Nevertheless, certain elements grow and entwine themselves in your life. Then, if you write about the elements all by themselves, you wind up writing about something lacking what it was that made them so good, that is, you.

When she was in fifth grade, my daughter had a textbook on what they called "self-esteem."

Recall something that happened to you yesterday or last week. You can choose to see and hear the things you did well. Or you can choose to imagine over and over and over the mistakes that you made.

. . . constantly recalling criticism can make you feel bad about yourself. Recalling the times you have been successful and the compliments you have received makes you feel good about yourself.

If you are like me and many other guys, you've never in your life recalled any of your good moments. What you have done is opt to recall the painful, horrible moments of your life. You like to spend whole hours, perhaps whole weekends, recollecting the times when you have behaved like a sea slug.

Any pathetic chance I might have had at self-esteem was taken from me at an early age. My first influence was the Philadelphia Phillies, years 1959-69. Self-esteem-wise, those years were like being locked inside the Bastille. The Phillies finished either last or almost last every year during that era. Other kids who liked better teams would pretend that they were Willie Mays or Mickey Mantle or Eddie Matthews. I would get up to bat and pretend that I was Clay Dalrymple.

No wonder my eyes were downcast. The best player on the Phillies was a guy named "Pancho" Herrera. I believe he hit seventeen home runs in one year, an astounding total for a Phillie of that era. Herrera's big dream was to "buy a big yellow Cadillac." He was a giant. Not among men. Among Phillies.

I grew up with severely limited aspirations. I would pretend like all boys that I was a major league baseball player, but unlike other boys who dream of hitting sixty homers or winning thirty games, I would dream of hitting .261, hitting eight home runs, and making only fifteen errors.

Eventually I found that this "Phillie outlook" spread to other areas of my life. Other kids would write essays about what they would do if they were president. I'd write essays about what I would do if I ever actually got a job.

I began to look around for role models outside of the

Phillies organization. I was attracted to Lazlo Toth for a while. He was the guy who started hacking away at *The Pieta* with a ball-peen hammer. After he was taken away, Toth said, by way of explanation, "I was destroying the statue because I am the son of God and that's not my mother."

Michelangelo could never be on the Phillies, but Lazlo Toth certainly could. I think he would make a good utility infielder. I think Antonin Artaud, the French playwright, could make an excellent Phillie. He believed, and told all of his friends constantly, that he had a headache whenever anyone in the world had an orgasm. Artaud also believed that there was a cadre of compulsive masturbators in South America, and if you were really his friend, you would go down to Bolivia and stop them because they were giving him such a headache.

I see Artaud as a mop-up MAN and a mid-innings reliever. Maybe a spot starter.

I can see Saddam Hussein in the front office, maybe a GM.

Every year my mother would buy me the Phillies yearbook. I would actually *ask* for it. I wanted to read insanely optimistic predictions for the upcoming year only to have them utterly crushed by late May.

The yearbook would always have an ad for Tastykakes on the inside front cover. Then it would say something like this on the next page:

> All in all, 19(fill in) was a year that the Phillies would rather forget. But there's a new feeling in the air. (fill in) and his coaches are looking forward to(fill in) WITH OPTIMISM. All around there's a feeling that this is the year that we turn it around.

I would read the whole thing cover to cover. I would think, yes, this is the year. Ken Walters or Roy Seivers or Tommy Tune is going to make a big difference. Now that we had Gus Triandos or Northrop Frye, we would be a team worthy of almost-respect. I never had wild dreams. I would get excited if

I thought that the Phillies might finish sixth.

Here's the kind of thing that got me really pumped up:

> (Phillies player) really showed what he was made
> of last year. While many players would have
> responded to all of the criticism, (Phillies player)
> really deserves a lot of credit just for putting up
> with so many critical comments on a daily basis.

I graduated from high school in classic Phillie form. I finished 488th out of 513 students in academic average. If you divide by eight, you can see that I was indeed in the cellar. I immediately got a minimum-wage job, digging graves in a cemetery. When I sat in that little office, at Calvary Cemetery, and heard about the nature of the job, I knew for sure that I was applying for a Phillies job. I knew that, in the world of the labor force, I was going to be asked to hit .220.

After that, I was a pizza delivery man, a job that had Ruben Armaro written all over it. Then I got married, but it was okay. I was still in the land of the Phillies. My wife, whom I married for her money, had thirty-five dollars. There was an eight-by-ten section of our living room that you could not walk on because if you did, you would fall through the floor. In the winter, if you sat in our living room, you would see smoke coming out of your mouth whenever you breathed.

We applied for foodstamps but were denied because my wife's mom, who spent approximately three dollars raising my wife, claimed her as a deduction.

When I came home from college, my mother told me that she had thrown away my baseball cards, which are now valued at about twenty thousand dollars. When I got a little forward and asked her why, she looked at me blankly and said, "Do you want ham for dinner tonight?"

This incident is eerily similar to the time the Phillies made Ryne Sandburg the "player to be named later."

But then almost everything is eerily reminiscent of the

Phillies. For me. I hope not for you.

Sir James Barrie said that nothing that happens to you after you are six years old makes any difference. There is a lot to be said for this view. On a personal level, the most significant year was 1961. That was the year that Roger Maris broke Babe Ruth's magic-sounding record by hitting sixty-one home runs. The Yankees that year were often compared to the best teams in the history of baseball. They won 109 games. They had *six players with more than twenty home runs*. Mickey Mantle and Maris alone hit 115 homers. They won the World Series with laughable ease.

They were not, however, the team I was paying attention to.

The 1961 Phillies were equally awesome, but in a different way. They broke records, for sure. They lost twenty-three games in a row. I experienced the whole thing because I watched every game on TV. Games that weren't televised, I listened to on the radio. When they had night games, on past my bed time, I got my sister's transistor radio and listened to the whole sordid thing with the radio pressed against my ear and the sound turned down.

The Phillies' announcer was a MAN named Byrum Sahm. His name had a strange, almost incantatory effect on me. I would repeat it silently in my bed. Syrum Bahm. Byram Sahm. It was mantra-like, in the summer, drifting off to sleep with the sound of a name that could not be a real person after the Phillies lost yet again.

Ten. Fifteen. How can anybody, no matter how bad, lose *every* time? Twenty. How can this be? I thought, perhaps, that this was the end of everything, all life. It went on and on, like that final noise before the last water finally disappears down the drain. I half-knew that *I was dead*.

Of course, as they (should) say, "You can't lose 'em all." After twenty-three games, they finally won one. It was the first game of a doubleheader. They lost the second game, but for two hours we had a winning streak.

I did not die. I went on to become the twisted, beaten individual I am today. I live far from Philadelphia, but I can tell you, right off the top of my head, when the Phillies are coming to town. I'll be there.

Why do I do this? Why am I drawn towards this thing, the Phillies? Although I am hundreds of miles away, I never really leave them. They are in my dreams, my thoughts. Though I walk through Paris on a warm spring night, a certain part of me is with the Phillies. Why can't I forget them, especially when they have caused me so much pain? So much pain early in my life when I was least able to deal with it. I should hate them. But even now I think of their line-up for next year, their pitching. What should they do? They need a starter. Where will they get a starter? They need a stopper. Where will they get a stopper? They don't need a catcher. I am so happy! They don't need a catcher! They already have a catcher! A good one! They have the best goddamn catcher in baseball!

MAN and His Deceptions

AS WE LOOK OVER THE VAST PANORAMA THAT IS MAN, we are able to discern at least two distinct varieties. One of the best places to observe this phenomenon is the coast of Maine in the summertime.

The MEN that live there are what I will call variety A. Variety A MEN are rather tall and heavy. They either have beards or rough-looking faces, or both. They usually have at least one visible scar. They like to smoke while they work, and they like to drink when they're finished. These MEN are fisherMEN.

In June, however, we begin to see the other type, variety B. These MEN frequently try to look like variety A, but they aren't fooling anyone. They try to dress like variety A MEN, but their attempts are doomed to failure. Variety B MEN have no visible scars. Their hands have callouses only at the base of the little finger—racquetball callouses. Yet, even though these variety B MEN have enough money to dress any way they want, they choose to dress like the variety A MEN, who dress the same every day because that's the way they've always dressed. This dress entails boots, a fisherMAN's hat, old jeans, old shirt, and a slicker. Variety B MAN spends a lot of money attempting to "be" Variety A MAN. Why is this? Why can't he be content to be who he is—a Variety B geek?

This question brings us to an essential quality of the species, MAN. MAN always wants to pretend that he's somebody else.

Many animals practice what is known as protective coloration. Animals that live in the bushes, for instance, often have skin with a camouflage effect. This disguise is intended to keep other animals from seeing them in the bushes and going over and eating them.

Protective coloration is just one way animals have of being sneaky. Take the walking stick, for instance. The walking stick doesn't even look as if it's alive. It looks like a stick. All this, again, in the interest of sneakiness.

How about sand sharks? They scrunch themselves down in the sand so you can't even see them. Then you step on them, and they turn around and rip your leg off. They don't even play that *Jaws* music before they eat your leg, either. They go to all this trouble just so they can fool you.

You might think that MAN, as a higher animal, has outgrown all of this nonsense. You might think that MAN is a straightforward, heads-up kind of organism that doesn't need to stoop to all these sneaky shenanigans. You would be dead wrong. MAN, despite his status as a higher animal, is as sneaky as they come. As a matter of fact, you might say that MAN is just about the sneakiest damn thing in the whole pantheon of creation. MAN is seldom what he appears to be. MAN will steal your socks while your shoes are still on.

I'm not saying that MAN uses protective coloring, and I'm not saying that many MEN scrunch down in the sand until you step on them and then jump out and bite your leg off.

What I am saying is that MAN is very rarely what he appears to be.

Consider the example of a MAN who, while not better than all MEN, was certainly better than most. I feel safe in saying that in every way that matters (morally, intellectually, spiritually, hat-size) this particular MAN was "better than the average MAN."

This was a MAN I knew personally, a MAN whom I grew close to. This was, indeed, the only MAN I've ever had sex with.

This MAN was, of course, me.

Yes, even I. Even I could not escape the stigmata of sneakiness that is the bane of MAN's existence. Since I am, quite admittedly, in a confessional mode here, allow me to come clean.

I must tell the world, now and forever, that I didn't really read Stephen Hawking's explanation of the universe, *A Brief History of Time*. I merely tried to give everybody, in a sad display of a human sort of protective coloration, the impression that I really *had* read it. I let everybody see me with it, and I guess some people actually got the impression that I had read it, especially after I looked them right in their eyes and said, "Yes, I've read it. I've read Stephen Hawking's *A Brief History of Time*. Have you read it? You should. It's really interesting."

This is, then, my tragic story of lies and prevarications and big bullshit and shameless mendacity. It's not a pretty story. But it's true. Sort of.

It remains, perhaps forever, perhaps ultimately, impossible, to establish with any degree of exactitude just when this story starts. I know I was in a mall in July in the late 1980s. It was right before I went on vacation. I know I bought some books. I know I bought them in a Waldenbooks. I know I paid cash. Try as I might, however, I cannot establish the precise date.

In time, I may be able to improve on the clarity of the picture and develop one single theory that explains in verifiable detail the whole nature of the situation. Here, I want to do just one thing: comment in clear language understandable to the layman, with as little mathematics as possible, the answer to one question: how long was that copy of Stephen Hawking's *A Brief History of Time* in my possession, and how many times and in what ways did I try to give people the impression that I actually read it, when in reality I never made it past page nine?

This is the subject of my inquiry.

Today I know that time is inseparably linked to the same nexus that governs other phenomena such as space and matter.

In this regard, I can say, with reasonable certitude, that my copy of A *Brief History of Time* spent most of its time in three very particular localities. These are:

1. My night stand. It spent approximately thirty-five percent of its time right next to my clock radio.

2. My coffee table. Here the picture becomes, once again, obfuscated. Its time here cannot be accurately determined, primarily because its presence was often obscured by magazines. I believe it spent at least a week underneath *Wrestling News*, but I am merely making an educated guess. I do know that when *A Brief History of Time* was visible, it was always face-up.

3. The beach. A lot of time it sat, somewhat sadly, in my beach bag right up against a large plastic shovel. On several occasions, however, I took it out, read the back, and replaced it in the beach bag.

Time is such a fundamental concept, so central to our day-to-day existence, that it is not an exaggeration to say that we have, in effect, taken it for granted. I know I have. But when I realized, to my lasting shame, that I had taken time for granted, I resolved never to do it again.

The memory is a poor mirror; it amplifies and obliterates in random ways. I find that, in all of my memories, I am present. And the presence of myself throws the entire process into a dark pit colored with emotion and turmoil.

I guess I was afraid, really, of what I was facing. I felt that if I opened and read that book, many of my most cherished ideas would be exposed as pseudoscientific mumbo-jumbo. I suspected as much already, yet I was afraid just the same.

Allow me to put it this way. I have just come out of the water and I am rubbing my head with a towel. Kenny, a friend, reaches into my beach bag and removes my paperback copy of *A Brief History of Time*.

"You readin' this?" he asks.

"Yeah," I say. I'm spreading some sun block on my nose.

Kenny turns *A Brief History of Time* over and reads the back.
"Any good?" he asks.
"Yeah," I say. "Real interesting."
"Everybody's reading that book," he says.
"I know," I say. "It's good."
Kenny puts *A Brief History of Time* back in the bag.
"I'm going back," he says.
"I'll see you back there," I say.
"See you," he says.

Einstein, of course, demonstrated that time is, in fact, elastic. It can be compressed and it can also be expanded. The same amount of time can be really long—fifty years, say—or it can be really short. All of this depends on other factors. Consider the incident I just described. Consider that each individual (here Kenny and I) carries his own sense of time around with him. A certain amount of time, to me, can seem much different from the same time in someone else's perspective.

Thus:

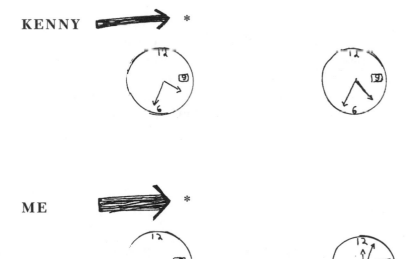

NOTE: *time's arrow

At one time, it seems almost ludicrous to remind ourselves, time was actually considered a pretty simple concept. You had forty-five minutes for lunch. You had to make sure to file your income taxes every ten years or so. Today, of course, we know that things are vastly more complex. When was the last time any serious, well-read person thought about things in quite so simplistic a manner?

Do you remember those quaint days when you thought of things as "over and done with"? Questions such as "What's the score now?" are no longer, for me, and for many other well-read people, such simple matters. After all, if you were in a space craft sweeping past Earth at close to the speed of light, I don't think that you would be asking me that question. Pardon me if I suggest that maybe you just might not be that glib about everything when I explain that a baseball on earth, from your perspective, would take several human lifespans to reach home plate and even then it's extremely doubtful whether the batter, probably Ken Griffey's great-great-grandson, would even swing at it.

We, of course, are a big mistake. That much I did learn during the undetermined time when *A Brief History of Time* was in my possession. We owe what little existence we have to a macromolecular era that allowed for the production of plentiful oxygen in the atmosphere. I love the way I say that. I happened to look at that sentence right before lunch. I could tell, even then, that it was a sentence that would come to mean a lot to me.

Allow me to explain.

I am eating lunch with a friend, Paulette. She has seen me "reading" right before lunch.

"Do you want any of this salad dressing?" asked Paulette.

"Yeah. That's the good kind, isn't it?" I replied.

"Yeah," she answered.

"You ought to read this book I'm reading," I said.

"Yeah, I saw you reading it. What is that book?" she asked.

"It's called *A Brief History of Time*," I said. "Pass me that pepper, will you?"

"I heard of that book," she said. "Any good?"

"Yeah, it's real good," I said. "Real interesting. Like I just read that the whole human race is really just a big macromolecular error. If it weren't for that, we wouldn't even exist."

"Let me have the catsup," she said.

Forgive me for relying, once again, on charts. Sometimes, to my regret, I find that words are an inadequate vehicle for certain complexities. The following, I think, makes my point rather clear:

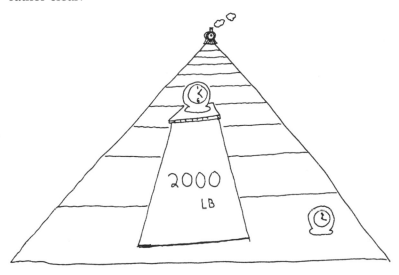

Change occurs, of course, because objects move about through space in time. Time doesn't move. My copy of *A Brief History of Time* does. It is difficult to determine with any degree of precision just when *A Brief History of Time* ceased to "exist" in my house and beach bag.

Today, of course, I know that "Where the hell is my copy of *A Brief History of Time*?" is a meaningless question. There is a symmetry between the past and the present. The second law of thermodynamics, for example, states that things become less and less ordered. Let's not mix epistemology with metaphysics because then we will become confused as hell.

But if you got my book, bring it back. I miss it.

I've been pretending to read *Ulysses*, but it's just not the same.

Iron MAN

LATELY, THERE HAS BEEN A NEW DEVELOPMENT CON-
cerning the subject of MAN. Many MEN have taken to going
out into the woods and beating on drums and weeping. We've
all done this, of course, at one time or another. I, for instance,
have gone into the woods, and I have wept, and I have beaten
on a drum. Yet I have never done all of these things at the
same time. I may have wept while beating on a drum. I might
have gotten really depressed during "Soul Sacrifice," for
instance, but, not surprisingly, I don't remember it that clearly.
I do remember weeping after my brother hit me with a drum.
That happened in 1957.

I have never beaten on a drum while in the woods. I have
cried while in the woods. As a matter of fact, I've cried almost
every time I've been in the woods. Who wouldn't cry? There
was no cable. Instead, there were insects. And larvae. Beau-
coup larvae.

The last time I was in the woods, I started sobbing uncon-
trollably, and I frightened several—what do you call it?— animals and whatnot. I knew when it was time to quit.

Now, big gangs of MEN are headed woodsward. They are

bringing stuff to eat, and, more importantly, they are bringing the drums.

On the surface, to the casual observer, this might seem to be a pretty lame movement. A casual observer might say something like, "Look at all these jerk-offs from my homeroom." That, however, is taking the easy way. It is all too easy to dismiss the early vanguard of a new and potentially revolutionary group. Especially if it happens to be a group that disturbs the comfortable, established values of a powerful group like MAN.

In writing this book, I have tried very hard to avoid the casual approach. Too much shoddy work slips by these days under the puzzling title of "scholarship." There seems to be a sort of cavalier air about much of what passes for "fact." "Let me get this down fast, before I have totally checked it," goes this line of so-called reasoning. "At least I'll get paid, and I'll be in Mexico before they find out that I was really only a 'casual observer.'" This kind of crap goes on all the time, so I made extra special positive that I wouldn't turn out to be one of those guys.

In other words, if you have the impression that the MEN's movement is really pathetic and stupid and involves a bunch of borderline cases wandering around jacking off in the woods, I'm here to tell you right now that you are all wrong. The MEN's movement isn't a bunch of borderline jerkoffs wandering around in the woods beating on drums and beating off, all the time moaning and bitching and wallowing.

It's really much worse than that.

Get rid of that Mary Poppins attitude and let's go inside the MEN's movement.

The basic idea behind the MEN's movement is that MAN is lost. The old ideas of what a MAN is—so goes this line of thought—are completely irrelevant to the situation that MAN finds himself in. To the MEN's movement, the old ideas about MAN are worn out and useless. To these guys, there is only one thing that you have to acknowledge.

You have to acknowledge that you have a *wound.*

This is not an obvious wound. Like a shotgun wound. No, this wound is really difficult to pin down. It's buried deep inside the MAN. Deeper than the islet of Langerhans.

So what do you, as a MAN, do about this wound? It's buried deep. It's buried so deep that it can't hear Jerry Lee Lewis, yet you're supposed to go looking for it. You're sitting there with a brewskie watching college football. You're over at another MAN's house, so you know you don't have to clean up. The refrigerator is packed with Heinekin. As you sit watching the game (Notre Dame-Michigan, let's say), you can smell somebody cooking some very large piece of meat in the kitchen. Next to you are other MEN who enjoy watching football. These are MEN that you have known since the days they enjoyed *playing* football—in other words, a very long time. Notre Dame, down by ten in the fourth quarter, runs back a kickoff for a touchdown. On the ensuing kickoff, Michigan's kick return specialist, an early season Heisman candidate, fumbles the ball. Notre Dame recovers the ball in the end zone. The clock runs out. The gun goes off. The crowd goes wild. It's a miracle. The greatest game ever, some say.

Miller time? No, time to start looking for the wound.

Right.

At this point, for illustrative purposes, I think it would be good to relate a personal experience, one that is certainly germane.

I do not seek to talk for all MEN. I leave that to Charlton Heston. Yet I am a MAN and it just occurred to me that I might function in an explanatory manner.

Like many MEN, I have often wondered just what it was to be a MAN. I knew that I wore pants and I had hair all over me, but that alone wasn't satisfactory anymore. I needed more answers, better answers. Being big and hairy just wasn't enough anymore.

I guess the last straw was getting on the little train thing that takes you to the Atlanta airport terminals. I had gotten on these things countless times, but this time I was the person being singled out when the little voice says, *The reason we are not moving is that someone is obstructing the entrance.* I had been on these trains hundreds of times. I had heard the voice, the electronic voice that tells the poor pathetic idiot to get his coat out of the door for crissakes. I had gazed over at the offending party and, along with the other reasonably intelligent passengers, smiled a little smile about the poor idiot with his pathetic coat caught in the door.

Now, I was the pathetic idiot. It was my coat caught in the door.

I got off the train okay, but I could feel the eyes of my fellow passengers burning into the back of my skull.

I got home to my home and there was no one home. No cheery little (dare I say it?) female voice. No martini. No nothing. Just a note on the refrigerator.

> TOOK THE KIDS TO A MOVIE. BE BACK
> AROUND ELEVEN.
>
> LOVE, PAULETTE

I had heard about the new thing in maleness, and I was itching to try it. This seemed like a pretty good time. It was eight-thirty, so I'd have an uninterrupted block of at least two hours. If I used my time well, I could get into some serious new male activities.

I walked out back and looked up at the moon. It was a very clear night and the moon seemed to be smiling down on me.

Yes, I thought, it's the MAN in the moon. He's smiling down on me. He's the MAN in the moon, and he likes what I'm doing. If I had to sacrifice something down here, in the interest of maleness, I was quite sure that my big buddy with the round yellow face would approve.

I got out this big empty can. Someone had sent it to me, filled with popcorn, at Christmas. I didn't even have to turn it over. The top sounded great.

I admit, I needed some help. MEN today are no longer afraid to ask for help. I turned to Carlos Santana. I got out "Soul Sacrifice" and I turned it up on my big JBL speakers, which I had bought years before I knew that it was really hard to be a MAN.

I stayed out there beating until my father, a.k.a. the moon, had turned not yellow. I looked up at him, and I am still relatively certain that he was still smiling.

After about an hour, after going through some "Teen Beat" records and Buddy Rich's "Love for Sale," I felt a lot better. A damn lot better.

It's very important for MEN to do this kind of thing. American MEN in the nineties need to do this every chance they get.

American MEN never get to sit out in the dark beating on a popcorn can drum. This is why we have so many problems. Why does the typical American MAN feel so senseless, so removed from his real role? What is his real role? Are we predators? Are we hunters? I know that we're not shoppers. Some of us may be foragers. I had a friend who was a forager. Did it make him happy? He didn't look happy the last time I saw him.

All I know is, I'm going to beat this drum. My hands turn into a blazing whirl of moonlit flesh and my sweat begins to pour in rivulets.

I'm a MAN. EM. AYE. ENN. If my coat is obstructing the doorway, I think you better come back here and tell me about it yourself, Jack.

There are many important things that MAN has forgotten. He has forgotten the wild MAN who lives inside him. He has forgotten the child within, who also lives inside him. Like Huck Finn he has started down the Mississippi, never realizing that he had these people, the wild MAN and the child, inside him. He has also probably forgotten his mother's birthday, and boy is he going to hear it about that. That's going to make MAN feel pretty bad.

To feel better, MAN has to become whole once again. He has to look at life through the eyes of a child. Any child's eyes will do, but it's not easy to get them. Your average child is not going to surrender his eyes on request.

Once MAN has remembered the wild MAN and the child that live within him, and called his mother who had begun sobbing, he is ready to start getting whole. First, give the kid back his eyes. You're finished with that. Now it's Gene Krupa time, time to go to the drums.

I like to start with a little shuffle beat, but that is up to the individual MAN. I then start to think Ginger Baker, "Do What You Like." Soon I'm thrashing. That's my personal plan, but each MAN has to experiment and find his own thing that makes him whole. Bongos? Sure. For some MEN. Congas? Acceptable under some conditions. Check with your local rules committee.

Act Like a MAN, A Real MAN

LET'S TAKE A MOMENT AND NAME SOME MEN. WHO IS the first MAN that comes to mind? John Wayne? Teddy Roosevelt? Dick Butkiss? Mike Ditka? Sonny Liston? Christine Keeler?

Everybody I just mentioned is a MAN, and it can be assumed that they all act or acted pretty much like MEN. They probably mowed a few lawns. They probably changed the oil. They probably stuck a little piece of toilet paper on their face when they cut themselves shaving, and they probably had to shave a lot because they all probably had really tough, MAN-type beards.

We *assume* all those things. However, as my ninth grade algebra teacher told me, "When you *assume* too much, you make an *ass* out of *u* and *me*. Ironically enough, it turns out that that nun was right on the money.

Consider this. When I was around seven years old, my mother took me to a movie called *The FBI Story*, or *The FBI*, or something. At any rate, while I sat their eating jujubes and looking up at the big screen, I formed one of my first impressions of masculinity. Surely, whatever else you could say about him, that tough-looking guy with the fedora who made hardened criminals pee in their pants was a MAN. No doubt about that.

His name, by the way, was J. Edgar Hoover.

What follows is an excerpt from some of his writings.

The death of many Americans has not brought any relaxation of Communists in America. If anything, it brought an increase in this type of subversive activity. The extent of the dedication of these masters of deceit is extraordinary, and it is difficult for the casual observer or layman to fathom just how deep all of this lies. Consider this recent interrogation that took place concerning a recent investigation into subversive activity.

Q: Would you prefer the Russians? Would you prefer the Russian system of government? That is, as opposed to the American form or system of government, that which we often refer to as democracy?

A: Could you make that a little clearer? I'm not quite sure just what it is that you are asking me.

Q: Do you like America? I don't know how I could put it any simpler? Now, answer the question.

A: Sure, I like America. But I would like to say, with your permission, just what it is that I like about it.

Q: Go right ahead.

A: I like America because every citizen has the right to express his own views. I like that, and I also like little, frilly lacy things that can be worn under one's clothing. I like the fact that you can be, say, a construction worker. Yet, if you feel like it, you can, under your Dicky's work clothes, wear a garter belt, a push-up bra, and crotchless panties.

Q: No further questions.

Subversive? That's what I called it.

Many of us find it difficult to understand how anyone who enjoys of the rights and privileges of the United States government decides to put on a bunch of Frederick's of Hollywood underwear and go out to labor as a rivet-catcher. But that's America.

One of the big problems with MAN is, then, that we can only see his outside. Outside he might have a nice tan, no hair growing out his ears, and a well-modulated speaking voice. He might be a nice guy—quick to lend you his lawnmower. He might be quick with a joke. When asked, he might even light up your smoke.

But that's only the part you see. When he gets home, he might be completely different. He might worship Satan. He might even read the *National Review*. If asked why he did these things, he might say "For the humor. It's a very funny magazine. Not to mention the works of Satan. They're very funny too."

MAN is very like a Pontiac Fiero. That was a car (they've all disintegrated by now) that *looked* like a "good" car. It looked a little like an Italian sportscar. However, inside it looked like Ronco's Italian sportscar. There was some foreign writing that you might mistake for Italian if you didn't know any better. It said, "Christ you're an idiot for buying this car. What did you think? They made a mistake and sold you an Italian sportscar for seven thousand dollars? God help you. Why any government allows you to exist is beyond me."

When someone tells you to "act like a MAN," just what is it that he's telling you? It has to depend on the MAN in mind. Consider the following hypothetical situation:

A MAN is crying. Another MAN looks at him. "Stop crying," he says. "Act like a MAN."

If both MEN happen to be thinking of Jake Lamotta (the obvious choice), there are no major problems. If, however, the two MEN aren't on the same wave length, trouble is brewing.

MAN: "Stop crying! Act like a MAN."

Other MAN: "Okay." (He goes outside and, with a beatific look on his face, begins very gently to feed the birds of the air. Soon birds have landed on his shoulders and hands, and he continues to feed them, his face radiant.)

MAN: "I give up."

This aptly illustrates the nature of the problem. The other MAN obviously interpreted "MAN" to mean St. Francis of Assisi.

This confusion occurs more times than most people are willing to admit.

How does one act like a MAN? It's relatively simple. The first thing to do is to adopt the correct attitude towards pain. Remember this sentence: "Pain is like the tooth fairy; only little babies think that it's real."

Another thing: learn how to tie a tie. Get out one of the reputable instruction books, or, for the more helpless, enroll in a night school course.

Then it's time to learn how to deal with women, your fellow creature on the planet. Bear in mind that there are two acceptable approaches when meeting an attractive woman. Look these two over and decide which one is right for you:

Method Number One: Look the woman up and down, then utter the following: "Oocha Magoocha!"

Method Number Two: Look the woman up and down. Then say, "Hey-ooo!" (Note: try to sound as much like Ed McMahon as possible. If necessary, consult old tapes of "The Tonight Show.")

A MAN should know how to talk. Memorize the following dialogue. It will prove helpful for those times when conversation is called for:

First MAN: "How about those Steelers?"

Second MAN: "Fuckin' A."

Still, when considering the question, how do I act like a MAN?, there's no avoiding the corollary: WHICH MAN?

This line of inquiry raises the topic of role models. The role model thing works like this: at an early age, you select another MAN, preferably older, and make him your model. You attempt to form yourself, after a fashion, in this other guy's image. Almost all MEN do this. So the choice of the role model is all-important.

My first role model was a gentleman named Joe Sauders. Sauders was in eight grade when I was in fifth. He had no discernible good qualities, but he had a cool walk. He would sort of rock and dip his right shoulder every time he took a step. As you might imagine, this technique caused Sauders to walk much slower than the average MAN.

I no longer walk like Sauders, but I notice, when I watch courtroom scenes on the local news, a lot of the defendants do.

After Sauders, my next role model was James Bond. I tried, whenever possible, while standing in the cafeteria lunch line or hanging around outside the Seven-Eleven smoking, to act like James Bond. I had read several of Ian Fleming's Bond books, and I had by that time seen both *Dr. No* and *From Russia with Love.* I wanted nothing more from life than to grow up resembling the tiger-muscled, Eton-educated, Secret Service-trained Brit agent whose life was nothing but danger, fast cars, beautiful exotic women, and Berreta-brand firearms.

Luckily enough, that's exactly the way my life turned out.

But this is all a little vague, isn't it? In this modern age we all want verifiable details. Facts. Numbers. For this reason, I offer the following test—a test devised by me and a bunch of scientists whose names are familiar to science fans everywhere. However, for obvious reasons, they have chosen, like Batman, to keep their identities a secret. Suffice it to say that they are all much smarter than you are, and they wear lab coats and everything and a lot of them are bald.

The credibility of this test is, then, without question. Though brief, it is an extremely insightful little exercise. After you take this test, you will know several things. Most important, if you are a MAN, you will know just how much like a MAN you happen to be.

DIRECTIONS:

Look at the following pictures. Then think: *what does that look like to me?* Be honest.

ONE

A. A TREE
B. A LAMP
C. AN ANGRY WOMAN
D. A VACUUM CLEANER
E. A SMITH & WESSON
    SERVICE REVOLVER

TWO

A. A REALLY HOT BABE
B. A VOLCANO ERUPTING
C. AN ANGRY WOMAN
D. A VACUUM CLEANER
E. YOUR MOTHER

THREE

A. A BUNCH OF MEAN AND
    NASTY SNAKES
B. YOUR TIES
C. SCARS FROM THAT TIME IN
    DA NANG
D. LACES TO YOUR BOXING
    GLOVES
E. LITTLE FRILLY, LACY
    THINGS

WHAT YOUR ANSWERS MEAN:

ONE: "E" is the correct answer. All of the other answers are okay except for "D." If you answered "D," you are a major wuss.

TWO: "A" and "B" are both good answers. "C" isn't that bad, although someone should keep his eye on you. If you answered "E" or "D," just go back to the book store and get the money back that you paid for this book. I'm not taking money from patsies like you.

THREE: "A," "C," and "D" are good answers. Damn good answers. This Bud's for you, *compadre*. If you answered "B," that's not that bad. I'm not going to dog you about it, but you might think about why you are walking down the road to weenieland with such a big smile in your face. If, however, you answered "E," just sit right there. I'm coming over, and I'm afraid that you're going to get worked. Sorry.

Entertainment
for MEN

WHEN IT COMES TO ENTERTAINMENT, THE WORD *MAN* has unfortunate connotations. When you hear "entertainment for MEN," your first thought is, I don't want that in my neighborhood. This kneejerk response is unfortunate because MAN is really a complex being whose tastes in entertainment are very diverse. MAN can enjoy an evening of *La Strada*. He probably enjoys three or four Bergman movies right in a row, especially after an after-dinner drink of fine French cognac or some sodium pentothal.

MAN's tastes in movies can't be easily summarized and dismissed.

The movies that people think of as MAN movies aren't really MAN movies in the truest sense. John Wayne, for instance, never made a movie with just MEN in it. From this perspective, *The Boys in the Band* is more of a MAN movie than your usual John Wayne cowboy movie. Chances are that John Wayne is dealing mostly with MEN (talkin' straight to them and occasionally hitting one of them). However, sooner or later Duke is going to run into Maureen O'Hara and either talk straight to her or spank her.

A couple of your real MAN movies, for example, are *The Dirty Dozen* and *The Great Escape*. To have a MAN movie, it's best to set it in either a prison camp or the army. *The Dirty Dozen* was about army prisoners who band together to carry out a dangerous mission behind the Nazi lines. *The Great Escape* was about a bunch of army prisoners who band together to escape from behind Nazi lines.

MAN's movies are popularly known as "action" movies. There is, as far as I know, no movie about a bunch of MEN who are prisoners of the Nazis, who, despite the differences in their national origins, are able to band together with their captors and set aside Thursday evenings for a discussion group.

When you think about action pictures, the same names come up over and over. Schwarzenegger. Stallone. Van Damme. Steve Seagal. Dolph Lungren. These guys are fine at what they do, but there's a vast, untapped audience out there, an audience that they're missing completely.

All of these guys have big muscles, big oily muscles. I don't know anybody with big oily muscles, and I'm betting that a huge segment of the movie-going public doesn't know any well-muscled, oily guys either.

Who do they know? More important, who can they *identify* with? I was having lunch last week with some people, and the talk got around to action films, and the subject came up: why aren't we seeing more actors that people can *identify* with as stars in action films?

The people I was having lunch with are people who produce movies. Movies you've paid money to see. Movies you've enjoyed. I'm not going to drop any names, but everybody at the table was a very powerful Hollywood producer. At least three were producer/directors. One was an actor/director/writer/producer.

On the way home, I had a thought. I pulled off the main road and headed over to the beach. I parked my car and got out. I walked down to the water. I sat down and watched the sun disappear into the ocean. One name kept repeating itself over and over in my brain. I knew it was right.

I had to develop an action film for John Sununu.

John Sununu. He enjoys music by Zamfir, master of the pan flute.

John Sununu. He's overweight.

I think that we can use both of these characteristics, and even feature them prominently in our prerelease trailers. Both of these are going to *connect* people to Sununu. They're going to be lined up around the block. Every fat guy with a Zamfir CD is going to be out there. There's a lot of demographics at work here, and we'll see that the first week we release the first Sununu action film.

The crucial thing to remember is that the vehicle is all-important. If we're going to cross over into mainstream on this one, we've got to have the perfect vehicle. We know that we're going to get the hardcore Sununu fan, the hardcore Zamfir fan, and the hardcore fat guy. That much is a given. What we want, and what we're hoping for, is the general moviegoer who might occasionally go to see a straight action film, but is probably not going to see one every week of his life until he is dead.

If we get that, we get everything. We're in the mainstream then, and we can put Sununu in a variety of roles and settings. He can even do *The Music Man* for all we care. But we have to get that first foot in the door. That foot in the door that leads to the mainstream.

There are a lot of other things that make me think that Sununu is a can't-miss action figure. I've never seen him without a tie, for instance. We don't even have to run the demos on that one. Everyday I see guys who don't know what their necks look like. Those are the guys we're going to get big-time.

I know what you're probably thinking. Isn't the action film thing over? Weren't the big movies last year little "gentle love story" type things? I say that you're overlooking a couple of things. It isn't action movies *per se* that are dead; it's just a certain *type* of action movie that's history. My Sununu project is going to open everybody's eyes.

The action movie I'm thinking about for Sununu isn't going to be a huge gamble. First of all, Sununu's not an established action star. Yet. We're not going to have to pay him like we would have to pay Arnie Schwarzenegger or even Steve Seagal. I think that if we approach Sununu in the right way—with sincerity and tact—we can get him to work really, really cheap. Also, we're not talking about a lot of hardware on this one. No exploding rockets or anything like that. We're going to need a nice big desk, a fax machine, some pens, some paper, and probably a lectern with a microphone for the scenes where Sununu ranks out some press guys. We're not going to need any alien spacecraft on this one, that's for sure.

I see a budget of $15 million, tops.

Sununu will be dynamite. I haven't even tested him yet, but I know in my gut that he's the guy I'm looking for. He's already got everything, really—a steely stare, a double chin, sensible shoes. All we have to do is capture him for the screen.

We do that, and we got $5,000 per venue as an absolute minimum. I think that Sununu might just go nuts and we wind up with an opening of ten per. It could happen. I can see it happening. As a matter of fact I can't see it not happening.

I think that we also have to consider a couple of other factors. First, there's the overseas market. I know Sununu is going to be a killer over there. Think of it. This MAN has a very unusual name. *Sununu.* I can just see a bunch of French action film fans pronouncing that name. I know they're going to love pronouncing that name. Nobody is going to say "John Sununu" in Frogland. It's going to be *Sununu,* period. Once they know you by just one name in Frogland, you are home free to the vineyards of megafrancs.

I'm not completely oblivious to 1990. I know what happened. But with Sununu, we've got a whole new sub-genre. I think that with some work, we can make Sununu extremely appealing to women ticket buyers, who are crucial. We want Sununu to be a "date movie" action figure. He gets very high scores on IQ tests, but more importantly, he can *project* that intelligence. This is the nineties and nineties women want smart action stars. A nineties woman is not attracted to big dumb guys with sweaty muscles who karate-kick people, but don't know how to talk about music and art.

A nineties woman, I'm betting, is a woman who can link up with a fat guy in a blue suit who went to college. I don't know anybody in this town who believes anything different.

> Summertime. The beach.
> "What you doing tonight?"
> "Kim and me going to the movies."
> "What you gonna see?"
> "I think we're going to see the Sununu thing. I
>   heard it was good."
> "I saw it last night with Krissy."
> "What did you think?"
> "Killer."

Try as I might, I can't not think this. That's how strong I feel.

Of course, television is the vast wasteland of MAN's entertainment. Except for ballgames and fights, there is precious little for a MAN to watch. This is an unfortunate situation, but the growth of Cable TV has created reason for hope. Perhaps, in the not-too-distant future we might see a cable network devoted to things that MEN want to see. I know what you're thinking: is he advocating another porno channel or another ESPN-type sports channel?

No, I'm not. I want a channel of entertainment for MEN. I've already thought this through.

IF JOHN FORD RAN THE FOX NETWORK

THREE BAD MEN. Grampy (Robert Conrad), Boone (Parnell Roberts), and Maydew (Fred Dryer) drink a bottle of

Jameson's Irish whisky and laugh drunkenly about life for thirty minutes.

HANGMAN'S HOUSE. Baggy (Scott Baio) kicks O'Brian (Johnny Depp) right in the ass. O'Brian gets up and challenges Baggy to a fight right then and there. Then "Thick Hide" (Chuck Conners) tells them that their father just died, and they put to rest any thoughts of fighting.

FOUR MEN AND A PRAYER. Baker (Doug McClure), Shamus (John Amos) and O'Toole (Jimmy Walker) are marooned on an island. They come across some natives whom they beat senseless and drive off. Baker takes a swig out of the native's liquor, makes a horrible face, and does a "spit take." The four MEN and a prayer share a laugh.

YOUNG MR. LINCOLN. Lincoln (Alan Alda) defends Armstrong (Robert Blake), who is accused of cowardice (refusing to bite the end off a cigar). Lincoln's eloquent plea results in a verdict of "innocent." Lincoln takes Armstrong off to the side and tells him to stop acting like a woman.

WAGON MASTER. Travis (Robert Urich) leads the Mormons to Crystal City, where they find, once again, that there aren't any women. Travis and Carrot Top (played by himself) smoke cigarettes and then throw them away when they are finished. Then Travis and Carrot Top beat their horses.

THE SIMPSONS. Marge convinces Homer that the family should convert to Catholicism, which they do. Bart becomes an altar boy, but he gets into trouble for eating handfuls of hosts and engaging in candle-snuffer "duels" with the other altar boys. Lisa and Marge say a Novena for him.

MAN and Woman

RECENTLY, BOOKS LIKE DEBORAH TANNEN'S *YOU JUST Don't Understand* explained to MEN everywhere the precise nature of their verbal communication skills. Consider this example.

MAN: I seen that picture of you with that big house with the columns. You said I was common. Oh how right you were! I'm as common as dirt! But I pulled you down off those columns and baby didn't you love it when we got those color lights a-moving and we could make noise in the night! And then she shows up all hoity toity, describing me like an ape!

Woman: Who do you mean?

MAN: I mean your sister, Blanche. You know your sister's no fairy queen. Yeah, some fairy queen she is! You know in Laurel, Dame Blanche is as famous as if she was the president of the United States. Except she's not respected by any party.

Woman: I think you should read Deborah Tannen's *You Just Don't Understand.*

MAN: Are you familiar with the Napoleonic Code?

Woman: A better question is, *Are you familiar with the male/female communication code*, Stanley?

This is a classic example of the different ways that MEN and women express themselves. Because of these differences, the MAN and the woman in this example are obviously experiencing a gap in communications. After some serious interpersonal therapy, however, things might be a lot more harmonious:

MAN: Oh, look at this picture, Hon! It's a picture of you standing on the porch of your old family house in Laurel. Isn't it darling? Those big white antebellum houses, they're just ravishing. Don't you think so, Hon?

Woman: I agree completely.

Yes, MEN and women are quite different. A few years ago, certain professions were practically all-male. Doctors. Lawyers. Engineers. All of these professions were dominated by MEN. If you talk to older women who happen to be doctors, for instance, they will tell you that they were perhaps the only woman in their medical school classes. A friend who is a surgeon told me that she is always asked where the doctor is. There used to be a little test to see how ingrained these prejudices were. It goes like this:

A MAN is dating and having sex with a doctor. Yet the MAN says he isn't a homosexual. The MAN lives on an island where everybody either tells the truth all of the time or lies all of the time. The MAN is standing next to another MAN from the island. This other MAN is a homosexual. As a matter of fact, he asks you if you know any MEN for him to have sex with. Both of the MEN are wearing argyle socks. Truth-tellers never wear the same kind of socks as liars.

Can you ask one question of one of the MEN and determine with 100% accuracy:

A) Which MAN is telling the truth, and

B) What island are we talking about?

It is in the area of sports where this sexual segregation most clearly still exists. There are no women in the National Football League. There are no women in baseball or basketball. There are no women boxers. There are also, as far as I know, no women referees. A woman referee in a boxing match might have a tendency to be kinder than a man, but this is, of course, quite debatable. There is no real reason why a woman couldn't referee a fight, although I can picture the contrast something like this:

A boxer has been knocked down twice. The second time he gets up, the referee looks closely at his eyes and asks him a question to see if he's okay.

MAN referee: "Are you alright?"
Fighter: (nods head)
MAN referee: "Okay, continue" (waves fighters together).

Woman referee: "Are you alright?"

Fighter: (nods head)

Woman referee: "What's the chief export of Brazil?"

Fighter: "I dunno."

Woman referee: "That's it!" (signals fight over)

My own feelings on this subject come from my own experiences which took place, I like to think, in my own life.

The first person I ever played what might be called "ball" with was my sister, and we played jacks. She kicked my ass. I wanted to play again, so we did. She kicked my ass again. I *begged* her to play just one more game with me, so she finally agreed, although she obviously had much better things to do. I had to plead with her to play just this one more game. We started to play, and I started trying to cheat very blatantly. She asked me, in a relatively polite manner, to stop cheating. I kept cheating. Finally, she couldn't take it anymore, so she just got up, called me a cheater, and ran up the steps.

I waited until she was almost at the top of the stairs. Then I said, "Mom! Mary called me a cheater!"

I've always been a sportsman, even from the very beginning. I guess it ran in my blood.

All too soon, however, my idyllic afternoons of cheating at jacks came to an end. I was older now. No longer would I cheat at jacks with my sister. Now it was time to be dishonest on a far grander scale. Some day, I hoped, I would be able to say that I had cheated at jacks with women in their eighties, perhaps older.

A dream? Perhaps. But I will go on dreaming. Some MEN dream. That's what they do. Some MEN see things as they are and say "Why?" Some MEN see things that never were and are checked into a facility and receive medication.

MAN and His Education

MAN HAS ALWAYS VALUED EDUCATION. ALMOST ALL MEN are, before venturing out into the world, "prepared" for what comes next. The education described as "formal" involves going off to a place where the students sit in little desks in front of a larger person in a larger desk, who is called the teacher. In time, many MEN grow larger than their teachers, but the desks usually stay the same.

This process is called education. Virtually all MEN find themselves engaged in this process for a period of time. The period of time, however, varies widely. William Faulkner never even finished high school. On the other hand, Donald Trump has a graduate degree from an Ivy League school. The case of Faulkner and Trump is useful for illustrative purposes. Which MAN wrote the "smarter" book? Could a MAN without a college diploma produce a towering work of intellect like *Trump: Surviving at the Top* or that scholarly opus *The Art of the Deal*? Of course he couldn't. And that's why school is all-important to every MAN. Consider all those little MEN out there watching NBC's "All-Star Stay in School Jam." Think of all the little Donny Trumps watching attentively as Sinbad explains the importance of education. Then think, tragically, of all the little Billy Faulkners who aren't paying attention. It's enough to make even a hardened MAN like me pause.

A few years ago, the number-one best-selling book of the year was a slim volume called *Everything I Need to Know I Learned in Kindergarten*. The idea was, essentially, just what the title says: all of the really important things that you've learned were taught to you when you were a little kid. These things turn out to be things like "If you hurt somebody, say you're sorry"; "Tell the truth"; "Hold hands when you go outside"; and "For God's sake, don't play with your own shit!!!" (I made that one up, but darn it, it seems like it belongs.)

Anyway, this guy's book made him a very wealthy man. I saw the guy on TV and he looks just like you figure he'd look. Beard. Gray. A little fat. Not terribly bright, but not pathetically stupid.

But my purpose is not to belittle this fat, gray, not terribly bright guy. As a writer myself, I certainly don't envy another writer who writes a stupid book that earns him much more money than any of my enormously clever books, written by the sweat of my brow, have earned me. Just because my family of adorable children have to go to bed hungry because people bought his pathetic garbage book instead of one of my books ("Rarely is a book whose wordplay is so dazzling this funny." — *Newsweek*, review of *Yo, Poe!*, by Frank Gannon, father of three adorable children.) No, I'm very happy for him. It always makes my heart a little lighter when a fellow humorist ("humorist," they call him) writes a book that sells really, really, well.

But allow me to say this. I HAVE thought of some things he left out of his list of "everything I need to know":

EVERYTHING I REALLY NEED TO KNOW I LEARNED IN BOOT CAMP

I, like everybody else, like to think that I know what's going on. That's why every February for a number of years I've sat down and tried to write down just what it was that I believed at that particular time.

I kept all of my old statements of what I believe, and recently I got them all out and read them and boy did they make me sick. One year I'm a pompous ass and the next year I'm a whining simpleton. I felt like taking those other versions of myself that wrote those statements of belief over to a lounge near the airport, getting them dead drunk, embarrassing them in public, and leaving them in the parking lot.

Then, just recently (since 1986) I noticed that the lists were changing in character. The person writing these lists was becoming terser, more compact. Closer to something. More recently still, I decided that I would get just really terse and compact, and I set about writing a statement of belief that would be no longer than one page, with margins, typed double-spaced with elite typeface. Then I chickened out a little and made it pica.

I knew that I would be considered naive, even stupid, by many. Yet I went ahead with it. My inspiration for this difficult task came on a very ordinary Saturday morning. I had just finished pouring Kay-Ro Syrup into my crankcase and I was ready to go into the house, wash up, and put the dog into the microwave.

Then it hit me: *Isn't everything a little bit simpler than we make it out to be?*

I realized that I already knew everything I needed to know. I had learned it a long time ago. And I didn't learn it at Harvard and I didn't learn it at Oxford. I didn't learn it at Stanford and I didn't learn it at Belmont Abbey. I didn't learn it at Blitz-Lube and I didn't learn in the back of my daddy's car.

I learned it at boot camp.

Here are the things I learned:

A HAIRCUT TAKES FORTY-FIVE SECONDS.

HAND GRENADES ARE YOUR FRIENDS.

IF YOU HUMP SOME 105mm CRATES AND BURN SOME FOUR-HOLERS EVERY DAY, YOU'LL BE ALL RIGHT.

A RECON TEAM OF SPIE RIG CARRIED BY A CH-46 WHILE GUNSHIPS PROVIDE COVER IS A BEAUTIFUL DAMN THING.

SPEAK ONLY WHEN SPOKEN TO AND MAKE THE FIRST WORD OUT OF YOUR MOUTH "SIR."

MAKE THE LAST WORD OUT OF YOUR MOUTH "SIR."

SAY "SIR" A LOT.

DROP AND GIVE ME TEN.

THERE'S NOTHING BETTER THAN AN AMPHIBIOUS LANDING.

I WILL UNSCREW YOUR HEAD.

YOUR NAME IS SALLY. GOT THAT, BOY?

GIVE YOUR RIFLE A GIRL'S NAME.

ONE, TWO, THREE, FOUR.

TALK TO YOUR RIFLE.

USE THE WORD "SIR" MORE OFTEN.

There it is. Everything you need to know is in there some-where. Goodness and beauty and truth and rationality and love. It's all in there. Aesthetics and ethics. Things we give fancy names to. It's all in there.

Everything's in there. Vegetable oils, resins, lubricants, inorganic matter. The whole thing. It's right there.

Take any one of those items and apply it to the frighteningly complex world we all live in. Suddenly, almost magically, it's not so frightening and it's not so complex anymore.

How much better the world would be if we all—the whole world—dropped down suddenly and did ten fast pushups. Or if everybody only had to wait forty-five seconds before it was his turn for a haircut.

Or if everybody took a minute out every day to talk tenderly, sincerely, to his rifle.

And it's still true, no matter where you are in life or what you happen to be doing, to look out over the coast and see an amphibious landing will absolutely transport you.

Cool MAN

THE BEST YEARS AND THE WORST YEARS IN THE LIFE OF
MAN often tend to be the same years. Charles Dickens, a
nineteenth-century MAN once wrote, "It was the best of
times, it was the worst of times." Almost all MEN, if they are
honest with themselves, will admit that they have said the following sentences many times on the very same day:

THIS IS GREAT!
THIS SUCKS!

However, the odds are best that the MAN who says these
particular sentences on the same day is a MAN who is somewhere between the ages of fourteen and eighteen.

These are rough years. They are also great years. These are
the years when you get pimples and have to take gym. But
these are also the years when you get to, for the very first time,
drink, smoke, and, perhaps, "get lucky."

Getting lucky involves, of course, girls. I think I have
already covered (excuse the expression) that subject in an earlier chapter. All forms of sex should be avoided by Catholics, of

course, but that is not what I want to talk about right now.

"Right now" is 1993. I haven't been eighteen for a long time. However, I can still remember what it was like to be a young MAN, and I feel that it is my moral obligation to say something about smoking, smoking between the ages of fourteen and eighteen. Smoking by young MEN.

Smoking is good. It's not only good. It's necessary.

But the writing is now on the wall. Soon there will be no more smoking in McDonald's, and not long thereafter that prohibition will be in force every place else. Most people find this gradual banning of all public smoking a good thing. Smoking is, of course, fairly bad for you, although many spokesmen in the tobacco industry dismiss such talk as "stupid rumors."

I do not call myself a scientist, despite several years of science in high school during which I maintained a "C" or better average. No, I am speaking here as a layman, and as a layman I feel that it's important to note that one issue is being overlooked in the anti-smoking fervor, especially the smoking-in-public issue.

It is impossible for a young American male to get through years fourteen through eighteen without smoking any cigarettes in public places.

Cigarettes, by the way, are never called *cigarettes* during the years in question. They are called, at various times, "smoke," "nails," "weeds," and my personal favorite, "butts."

With this rich variety of terms at hand, it is quite possible to go through years fourteen to eighteen without saying anything *else.*

For evidence, here is a list of everything that I said on the day of January 23, 1968.

"You got a butt?"

"Got any butts?"

"Give me a butt."

"Yes, officer."

"Got any matches?"

Before we go any further with this anti-smoking hysteria, we should consider a few facts.

It is virtually impossible to look bored and cool when you are a male of the age in question without a cigarette dangling from your lips.

Without a cigarette dangling from his lips, a male of that age group would be forced to admit to himself that he really is a male of that age group.

All known cool guys smoke. James Dean, James Bond, and probably (listen to "It's A Man's World") James Brown. Marlon Brando smoked. So did John F. Kennedy. Sinatra, it goes without saying, continues to smoke.

Now let's look at the list of non-smokers. Bishop Fulton J. Sheen. Roy Rogers. Pinky Lee. I rest my case.

What do you do with your hands? You can't put them in your pockets, lest someone accuse you of playing "pocket pool."

What are you going to do when, like every other Friday night of your life, you wind up at a Waffle House? Are you going to eat for three hours?

Do public policy-makers really want to deny some young MAN the intense pleasure of leaning over a pool table to make a shot with a cigarette hanging out of his mouth? The smoke comes up into your eyes, your eyes start to burn and water. You miss the shot, but you are cool.

I am quite sure that whoever is in charge of this public health lunacy would do well to think about those days when perhaps he too had pimples, perhaps he too walked through the minefield that is American male life in the years fourteen to eighteen. Perhaps he might change his mind about nails, weeds, and my favorite, butts.

So, with the aid of cigarettes and a few key phrases, MAN

can attain to a state of coolness that lasts until he is perhaps eighteen years old. After that, things get a lot more challenging. Eventually, every MAN reaches the state at which his deepest fears lie. He reaches the unthinkable, the antimatter universe of coolness.

THINGS THAT YOU HAVE TO DO THAT YOU CAN NEVER BE COOL DOING.

Buying insurance.
Mowing your lawn.
Talking about your house.
Looking at that hair that has started to grow out of your ears.

Competitive MAN

MAN IS PROBABLY THE MOST COMPETITIVE OF ANIMALS.
Consider a particular competition that pits MAN against
"lower" animal: a bullfight. Here we see the true nature of
MAN. When MAN wins, what does he do? Shake hands? No,
he prances and bows and picks up some of the flowers that the
crowd throws him. Talk about rubbing it in. They probably
never have interviews like this.

> "We're talking to Miguel Pistolera who, if you're
> joining us late, just killed Ferdinand. First of all,
> Miguel, congratulations on your win."
> "Thanks, Jorge. Ferdinand is a good fighter. He
> was tough. He gave me a good workout. He's a
> tough kid. He's got a future in this game."
> "He's dead, Miguel."
> "If that's what he wants. But it's a shame because
> he's a very skilled fighter, but if he's dead, then I
> guess that's his decision. I gotta hand it to him,
> Jorge. Very game kid."
> "Now let's talk about the fight. It looked like he

gave you trouble early."

"He did. But I just stayed with my fight plan, and, luckily enough I got a chance to ram that sword into the back of his neck. After that, it was just a matter of time."

"Thanks for coming by and good luck."

"Adios."

Man is a competitive animal. Just how deep this instinct lies is not always acknowledged. From the time when he is a little MAN, he is told to do " best that he can." But this concept—"the best that he can"—has no meaning without other MEN that he can "beat" at something.

The Olympics are just the most obvious manifestation of MAN's need to beat other MEN at something. Consider a book like *The Guiness Book of World Records* and you see that MAN wants to beat other MEN at everything. He wants to eat more hot dogs. He wants to drink more beer. He wants to memorize more words. He even wants to sit absolutely still longer than other MEN.

The desire to go "Nyahh, nyahh" to other MEN is perhaps the most primal urge of the animal MAN.

The Literature
of MAN

LITERATURE IS SOMETHING THAT MAN HAS, FROM TIME
to time, dabbled in. Indeed, more MEN have opted to write
literature than I could possibly list. Let me just briefly fill you
in on some of the major MEN writers.

For me, and for most MEN, when it comes to literature the
only MAN worth mentioning is the MAN from Oak Park. Not
that MAN. Ernest Hemingway.

Hemingway wrote just like a MAN. It's difficult, for
instance, to imagine Bess Myerson writing this:

> In the early days I'd fight anybody because I was
> hungry. If you're hungry enough, everybody you
> look at is a meal ticket. I was big and fast in those
> days. I had dark eyebrows and liked to wear
> wingtips. I'd just randomly select a number out of
> the phone book. Then I'd make the guy buy me din-
> ner. I didn't care. I was too hungry to care.
>
> In those days we rode the rails. It took a nickel to
> get inside the refrigerator car, but I never had that
> nickel. The refrigerator car was thirty-two degrees,

but it was a lot nicer than riding the rails.

Every night a guy would walk down the rails looking for guys who were riding the rails because they didn't have the nickel to get into the refrigerator car. You could never go to sleep when you were riding the rails. If you did, you'd fall off and a twenty-nine ton railroad train would ride right over you. If you were lucky enough to not fall asleep, that guy who checked to make sure that you paid your nickel would come around and you'd wish that you had fallen asleep and had a twenty-nine ton train crushing your body.

Like I say, I was hungry. That's when I got a call about a fight. Kid named Gargantua. Never heard of him, but my end was eight thousand: my only questions were where and when.

They wanted me for the middle of September. AC.

I said that that was no problem as long as they sent half of it by the end of August.

I asked Benny Leonard one night if he had ever seen Gargantua.

"Just in the gym."

"What's he like? Is he a hooker?"

"No. Jab. Jab. Jab. Straight right hand."

"Body?"

"He likes to go after the body with the left." Benny Leonard said hello to an Amish woman. I stood and smoked while Benny Leonard talked to the Amish woman. I had seen her at fights but I didn't know her name. Somebody told me she liked to quilt.

The Amish woman went away. Benny Leonard watched me watch her go away.

"She quilts?" I said. Leonard gave me a funny look.

"They all do," he said.

"You won't have any trouble with Gargantua."

"What makes you so sure?"

"You're intelligent. You'll left hand him to death."

I was a big MAN and only a big MAN can hope to get in there with a gorilla. Not just a gorilla, either. Any big hairy thing with an unusual name. A man, every man, if he's honest with himself, knows that he's secretly afraid to get in there with some kind of large hairy ape-like animal.

Men that really aren't afraid never talk about it. Then, once in a great while, they'll run into another MAN who is obviously not afraid of getting in there with a big hairy violent animal of some sort. When that happens, no one says anything.

I knew that I was a big MAN and I was not at all afraid for me. I knew that I could punch to the body, and I doubt very much whether a large animal with hair all over its body would know how to punch to the body.

The night before the fight, I couldn't sleep. I never can. It wasn't the monkey I was worried about. Me and Jack sat outside and looked at the lake. Nobody said anything for a long time. Then Jack said, "Well, tomorrow it will be all over."

I wished I could sleep. Jack said that Irishmen don't sleep. Jack also said that orangutans, gorillas, and greater lemurs can't sleep worth a damn either.

"Now an Armenian," said Jack, "an Armenian will sleep like a goddamn baby."

Me and Jack got up and walked inside.

"This is a rough business, Jack."

"You're telling me."

"Maybe I should have been an Armenian."

"Goodnight, pal."

It was a pretty good crowd. Lots of familiar faces.

The west side Irish. Plenty of Armenians. Also, a bunch of greater apes had charted a couple of buses. There was a whole section that was nothing but gibbons and chimpanzees, and gorillas were all over the cheap seats. I even saw some spider monkeys and I hadn't seen a spider monkey at a fight in a long time.

Teddy taped my hands and sprinkled paprika on them, just the way I like. Then he put on my gloves.

"This guy is easy to hit," Teddy said.

I got up and nodded. Eddie put a towel on my shoulder. Then he put on my robe.

"Let's do it," I said.

The ring looked a long way away. The crowd was very loud. I could see Gargantua just getting into the ring. I could tell that a lot of people who weren't greater apes were cheering for him. I'm an Irishman and an Irishman will always get a pretty good hand anywhere. A gibbon will get a really big hand, but only if he's fighting in his home town. I've never heard an orangutan get a big hand. People come to the fights for action and they're not interested in seeing an orangutan grab and hold for twelve rounds.

The referee was a Frenchman. I like French referees, always have, always will. They're not like a Dane. With a Dane you don't know what you're doing.

The referee says that we know ze rules and we better obey ze rules. I stick out my right glove and the gorilla slaps it. Teddy gets my robe and I wait for the bell. In the other corner Gargantua is on his toes snapping the jab. I lean on the ropes and wait.

At the bell he comes right at me. We trade jabs. He's got a good jab, but he keeps his hands low, like most gorillas. Teddy told me that if he could find a gorilla who could keep his left up, he'd marry him.

Near the end of the round I was short with a right
hand and Gargantua hit me with a left hook and I
went down.

I looked over at Teddy. I shook my head to show
him I was all right. I was all right. Gorillas are all
the same. They eat mostly vegetables and fruits.
They're not going to take you out with one shot.

The next ten rounds looked like the same round.
I'd be jabbing and moving. He'd be pounding away
at me and eating fruits and vegetables. The decision
was no surprise. I shook his hand and wished him
good luck. I knew right then that I was through. I'm
not going to stick around fighting pandas in eight-
rounders.

I said goodbye to everybody and left the auditori-
um and walked back to the hotel in the rain.

THE END

As far as I know, this story has never been collected. Which
startles the hell out of me because it is such a great, towering
story, a story that shows Hemingway at the very top of his
game from a MAN perspective. It is taut. It is superbly con-
structed. It is filled with poetry and yet it seems understated
and perhaps suggests more poetry that it actually delivers. It
carves itself as it goes along. It is impossible to imagine it exist-
ing in any other form and even if it were possible who would
want another form because this one is so taut and sculpted that
it almost seems that it's going to rip its shirt right up the back.
It is, finally, a great, great story, a good great story, a very fine
story and a story that will be here for other MEN to come
across in the future and say, "Great good goddamn story."

Today we all miss Ernest. We don't have a MAN like him
still writing. Some say Norman, but that's kind of a sad joke.
Ernest wrote good. Norman once wrote good but then he lost

it and started to write bad. Then he got it back and he started to write good. What good does it do to tell a writer to write good? If he wants to write bad, then that's just the way it goes.

I remember the last time I read Norman. It was bad writing. He was writing bad. I gave it to Steve and Steve read it and told me that it was bad and we had drinks. Steve was tight and I was cockeyed. We went out into the street where they kept the car.

"Norman writes bad, Steve," I said.

"I know he writes bad."

"It's a goddamn shame."

I went into the cantina and Steve went into the cantina and I became drunk. I became drunker than I have ever been. Drunker than I ever remember and my mouth was dry and I went home from the cantina and when I woke in the morning I ate a Slim Jim and bought a book by Brett Easton Ellis and it was written bad too.

So Ernest is gone and there can never be another Ernest. However, if Ernest were still here, he might be writing something quite a bit different.

Consider this:

You are tired all the way through. The fish is landed untouched by sharks and you have a bottle of Ballantine cold in your hand and drink it cool, light, and full-bodied, so it tastes good long after you have swallowed it.

ERNEST HEMINGWAY (actual Ballantine
Ale magazine ad from the fifties)

Or this:

THEIR SKIN WAS BROWN IN THE SUMMER

In the summer the people came and they wore Bain de Soleil and they drank the *Borrachera* and sat in the plaza. They did not get the sunburn because of the Bain de Soleil so they sat out and drank the *Borrachera* for many hours.

We had many wonderful afternoons. There was a barmaid there who we called "Squinty," and she would bring us *Borrachera* even when we ordered something else.

When it rained there was a softness and we would sit on the portico and smoke and talk about sunblock and how good Bain de Soleil was because it was without grease and it would not get in your eyes and yet it felt light on your skin and you would forget for a while the smell of cordite and the other things.

And later that year the soldiers came and their marching stirred up the dust that hung in the air and soiled the trees along the Rue d'Basque Jai Alai. We sat in our rooms then and talked about Picasso and I was impartial and we all had great color. That was a long time ago.

I left the beach and walked back to the hotel in the rain.

THE END

Not all MEN writers write prose. Some write in a form that they call poetry. Most MEN don't know anything about poetry. No one has established the exact reason for this sad state of affairs, but it may have a lot to do with MEN, at a young age, being forced to recite "Flower in the crannied wall, / I pluck you out of the crannies, / I hold you here, root and all, in my hand." I don't think that any MAN can be expected to even go on with life after being forced to say that in front of a group of his peers. I remember reciting Robert Frost's "Stopping by Woods on a Snowy Eve" to a group of my peers. It went all right until I said, "My little horse must think it queer."

After that, what's the point of going on? Yet a quick check reveals that MEN are still continuing to write poetry. I recently (much to my surprise) discovered a poet that MEN can actually appreciate.

REASON FOR HOPE IN AMERICAN POETRY

American poetry, as we begin the nineties, seems to lack direction. Most of our younger poets seem dominated by a tonal habit of despair. Many of our largest newspapers no longer review books of poetry. Much contemporary poetry seems landlocked in a sort of fashionable ennui. Indeed, most literate Americans could not name ten living American poets. The average literate American could, however, name ten or twenty or fifty professional athletes. Although the current situation in America seems to scream "BABYLON!" it is not yet time to throw in the cultural towel. There is a new voice on the poetic horizon, and everybody knows this voice. They might not know this voice as a poetic voice, but that's just what it is.

It is the voice of Hershel Walker, running back of the Philadelphia Eagles of the National Football League.

Most of you know Walker as a football player. Some of you may know that he writes poetry as a sort of hobby. But I am here to say that Walker's poetry writing is far more than a hobby, far more than an avocation.

Indeed, Walker may indeed be the voice of a generation, the voice that breathes life into this once-thought-dead art.

Walker's poetry reveals a delicacy and beauty that is remarkable in an artist who is so young (thirty-two) and so big (six-one, two-twenty). Consider these lines from his hauntingly beautiful, "I Can Not Say No":

It may be hard, but maybe one day I'll see
The world is not what it used to be.
It starts with a tear in your eye,
Next, you cannot say goodbye.

This is both savory and chilling, illuminating in its breadth of subject and the quiet tightness of its intensity. In only four lines Walker gives us the large ("the world") and the small ("tear," "your eye"). Poetry has been called the art of a fine excess, and that's just what we're getting here with Walker.

Randall Jarrell said that a poet is one who stands in thunderstorms for a lifetime and manages to get hit by lightning some half-dozen times. One look at Walker's oeuvre convinces the reader that this running back spends most of his free time out on the poetic golf course of his mind:

> The hurt has hit now with all its force
> I sit here thinking of you, of course.

Walker renders the world with a fidelity to the way things really look to him. He has an attentive quality that is obvious throughout the form and content of his work. Walker's is, more than anything else, a human voice. Like all human minds, Walker's sometimes explores the dark territories of the soul:

> You sit around the house and wonder
> You also think in bed
> Some days are bright, but most
> You wish you were dead.

This is no trendy, faked-up nihilism we're hearing here. This MAN really means it. Anyone can tell that. It's obvious.

But there are many facets to Walker, as indeed there are to any major poet. He can be as sassy and upbeat as the next major poet. Walker has more keys than a piano and, like a piano, not all of his keys are black ones:

> It is more than what I thought people would be
> Please remember me when it is time for you to leave
> I know I will remember you, keep in touch too
> For all you have done, Thank You.

These lines are filled to overflowing with ironic self-knowledge. Walker revels in his ability to find harmony in an unharmonious universe, and we go ahead and revel with him. In a universe where it is all too often "time for you to leave," Walker finds solace in the fact that we can all tell the leaver to "stay in touch." In a time of rampant selfishness and Trump-style avarice, Walker's voice is a voice of sanity and reason. Maybe we should all strive to "stay in touch" with Walker. We could do far worse.

Walker is, of course, not an easy poet to understand or appreciate. What really great poet is? Yeats? Pound? Eliot? Of course not. But Walker's complexity *is* organic. He is a rich alloy, a mixture of many things, many aspects, many experiences, many views, many things. To simplify Walker is to reduce Walker. That would be a shame. As he himself tells us in perhaps his greatest poem, the unforgettable, haunting, "They Do Not Know":

> I wish they could see
> The real person in me
> Some day I reckon they will know
> I'm not only here for the show.

The reader *must* ask, why *is* Walker here. Indeed, why are any of us here?

Walker's poetry is magnificent in every conceivable way: style, form, content, all are handled with the sure hand of the master. I know about these things, so trust me. Although most people know Walker only as a sports superstar, the time has come for us to see him for what he really is: a truly meaningful, truly original poet. Perhaps it is also time for all of us as a nation to put down our sports pages and pick our slim volumes of verse, or thick volumes. If you get 'em, start readin 'em.

So much for famous MEN writers. Ernest and Hershel are, after all, famous. Everybody knows at least one of Hemingway's novels. I've read *The Sun Also Rises* at least ten times. It was a good thing, too, because the first nine readings I didn't notice that Jake Barnes had a really serious problem. I have had my tonsils removed, so you could say that I could empathize with Barnes. He was in Paris missing something. I was in Winterville, Georgia, missing something.

Every schoolchild will one day probably be forced to memorize one of Walker's poems. Many eighth graders in the Jetson-like future will be quietly astonished to hear that Hershel Walker, the poet, was actually a well-known professional football player.

■ ■ ■

EXCERPT FROM THE NORTON ANTHOLOGY OF LITERATURE C. 2087

Walker possessed an eccentric genius. His very life was a dichotomy—somehow befitting the author of "I Can Not Say No." Walker was, for a time, a mountain climber, a lecturer at Oxford, and, we are always startled to remember, a professional football player. A look through a list of Walker's personal friends is a virtual catalog of his astounding versatility. Bob Hope. Norman Mailer. Bert Bacharach. It can be said, without fear of contradiction or error, that Walker knew the seminal minds of his epoch (1960-2051).

What about those MEN writers who are never going to turn up in Norton's Anthology of Literature? I feel for those bastards. Writing and writing, yet always knowing *no shot at the Norton Anthology of Literature for this honcho.*

Red Smith once said that writing was easy; you just sit down at your desk and open up a vein. I've tried it, along with many other things. It worked for a while, but then I got all woozy.

Nobody said that writing was easy. It's actually much easier to be a steel drivin' MAN than it is to be a writer. I've tried both, and driving steel is a piece of cake. I'd much rather stand in the hot sun with a forty pound hammer and a bossman without no soul. That's *much* easier than sitting in an air-conditioned room drinking bottled water and typing words on a piece of paper.

Writing is just so hard, in fact, that from time to time every writer asks himself why he bothers with it in the first place. Why not just be a lawyer or work at a Starvin' Marvin instead? It's got to be easier. Speaking personally, hardly a day goes by when I don't think that standing in the hot sun with a forty pound hammer and a bossman without no soul doesn't strike me downright appealing.

At times like that, I like to refresh myself by remembering just how horrible writing can get. I like to think about the real horror stories: writers who had just really bad things happen to them. Writers who just really got screwed.

Then I always feel a little better. Suddenly that John Henry, driving-steel-and-sweating-like-crazy life just doesn't sound that great. Suddenly, everything's back in perspective.

I think, again, of William Shakespeare. Did you know that he was dead and nobody had even published his work? Work that today almost everyone accepts as good work? Cervantes? They put that guy in jail. He writes *Man of Lamancha* and they throw him in jail. Unbelievable.

And it's not just writers who lived a long time ago and weren't American. Lots of American writers wrote really excellent things, and nobody paid any attention. Poe. Nathanael West. Melville. All of these guys were writers who got screwed.

The writer that I want to talk about isn't quite as well-known, but he, too, got screwed big time. The writer that I want to talk about, and the writer whose horrible story inspires my own work, is Jack Bitkoff.

Today people don't even know who Bitkoff is, but in the twenties, Bitkoff was a monster. If you look at any menu today, you'll see Bitkoff's influence. At one time, Gertrude Stein, Ezra Pound, T. S. Eliot, Howard Johnson, the Waugh Brothers and Jack Lalane all wrote paeans to Bitkoff.

Bitkoff was born in 1902 in New York City. His family, immigrants, I think, ran some sort of small family business. Bitkoff's childhood was remarkable only in its ordinariness. He was in his early twenties when he was asked, by someone we don't know, to write a description of the various cocktails that were available at a small restaurant in Greenwich Village.

The rest is history.

> Pina Colada:
> *Hey Mon, this drink be jammun*

> Frozen Strawberry Daiquiri:
> *So fresh, it should be slapped*

> Margarita:
> *The Gulp of Mexico*

At first, oddly enough, Bitkoff's work was largely ignored. Although schoolchildren today routinely memorize Bitkoff's drink descriptions, only a few really good writers noticed that Bitkoff had actually created a new literary genre.

E. M. Forster said that "although Bitkoff's drink descriptions embody what Matthew Arnold called 'spontaneity of consciousness,' and everyone seemed to recognize that right away, even before our orders arrived, I think that no one fully grasped how far he could go within the confines of the genre he had just invented."

The world was soon to find out, when it ordered dinner.

> 20-ounce T-Bone:
> *If steaks were states, this one would be Texas. It's big, lean and tender. This is a real meal, a meal to remember.*

Today, sadly, Bitkoff is virtually gone. Except in certain rari-
fied, bibliophiliac circles, his name brings little more than
raised eyebrows and scratched heads. The MAN who wrote
that timeless T-Bone description, along with so much else, has
been reduced to a footnote on a really thorough menu.

Is writing really worth it? I try hard to make some kind of
sense out of Bitkoff's sad fate, but I can't. I can't without lying
to myself. A damn good writer got screwed, but at least it
wasn't me. That's what keeps me going.

■ ■ ■

When I was back there in school, we used the NORTON
ANTHOLOGY OF LITERATURE to study samples of all
these famous writers' work. They were arranged chronological-
ly, so if you cracked the book real thin, you'd step right into
Beowulf land. Up to about page forty or so, there would be pictures of guys with swords and weird Anglo-Saxon helmets. You
open the book in the middle, you would see little guys in white
powdered wigs. If you went for the back of the book, you'd see
guys that looked pretty much like you and me.

But you could count on one thing. Out of all that writing,
there wouldn't be one single piece written by a woman before
page eight hundred. Then you'd get a little Virginia Woolf, a
little Marianne Moore. But as a whole, that big thick book was
packed full o' MEN.

Today, everything is different. Today's school anthologies
have women all over the place. I guess this is how it should be.
Women are, after all, our fellow-creatures-on-the-planet-that-
we-have-been-neglecting-lately. They should be able to write
anything that a MAN can write.

However, one last bastion of maleness still exists in the
world of words. Let's call it the "dot-dot-dot" genre. As far as I
know, no woman has ever been a "dot-dot-dot" writer. Women
should probably take that as a compliment because "dot-dot-
dot" is the lowest totem on the writer pole.

Let's imagine that there was only one example of every genre preserved for our distant posterity. What follows is the *platonically ideal "dot-dot-dot" piece written, of course, by a MAN, and I might be so bold as to call him "the MAN"*:

It's my dime . . . Isn't it true that everyone in America knows someone who has shot somebody and is proud of it? . . . Is it just me or does everybody smell funny right after they get out of the pool . . . Doesn't Bill Clinton remind you of some guy you punched in the mouth in a Holiday Inn lounge in the early seventies? . . . Everybody is thinking it but nobody's saying it, so let me be the one. That MADONNA is really acting like a slut or something . . . What the hell is a free range chicken? Can somebody help me out here? I've been all over America and I've yet to see a herd of chickens running around out there . . . Why is it that nobody smokes in restaurants anymore? I miss it . . . For my money nothing smells better than liquid paper. Nothing . . . Don't you hate it when you read that another celebrity has a spastic colon? . . . We wouldn't even *have* a drug problem in America if everybody would just relax, pour themselves a tall one, and put on some Sinatra . . . I know leather when I see it, thank you very much. So keep your vinyl-based products at home in your refrigerator or wherever you keep them . . . Try Tylenol. It's cheap, gives you a good buzz, and you feel a lot better the next morning . . . What the hell ever happened to Gabe Kaplan of "Welcome Back Kotter" fame? Let's hope he's not hanging around with those "Different Strokes" people. He was a giant . . . Is there any better feeling than waking up on a Sunday morning and seeing the mouse you've been chasing for a week caught by its neck in the trap? . . . Will somebody please tell me what it is with these rock groups and their names. Last week I saw an ad for a group called "George Bush's Large Intestine." This whole thing beats the heck out of me . . .

MAN and God

THROUGHOUT HIS HISTORY, CERTAIN QUESTIONS HAVE bedeviled MAN. Why do the innocent suffer? Why do those who are good seem to experience more pain than those who are bad? Why can't the bad be more like the good? Or why don't the bad at least apologize or at least *look* worried?

I have tried to help my fellow MAN in his quest for these answers. After I learned that there was no answer sheet, though, I swiftly gave up. When I was younger, a younger MAN, I had a two-fold approach to the big questions. This consisted of—

    ONE: SHOOT.
    TWO: HOLLER "SHIT."

Now that I am an older MAN, I find things much more complex. There have been many furrowed brows and many all-nighters with a lot of coffee and butts and trips to the bathroom. I no longer "take things for granted." Now, as I look at the spots on the back of my hands (liquid paper, it turned out), I realize that life doesn't last forever, and I better start thinking very hard about things like this story, which is true (except for certain understandable changes, such as the names of the characters, and the details of the story).

Al and Bob were identical twins who lived in Wisconsin. Although they looked exactly alike, they couldn't have been more different. Al was a model son. He got A's in school, and was captain of the football team. He didn't drink or smoke, and when he married Mary Ann Johnson, he was still a virgin. Al graduated first in his class and went on to Johns Hopkins for medical school. He had three wonderful children, two girls and a boy. His son, Al Jr., was a junior olympic skater who was also captain of the football team and an academic All-American. Al's two girls were beautiful, intelligent, and talented. All three children loved Al.

Bob, however, was a different story. Bob was a "bad egg." He failed school all the time, but showed no remorse or interest. Bob thought that a good day was a day spent stealing those little March of Dimes coin boxes from Seven-Elevens. Bob wouldn't even feed his own dog; he forced it to go kill its own food in the neighborhood. Bob slept with lots of girls. He got three of them pregnant, yet he refused to accept any responsibility for his actions. He never bought anyone presents at Christmas, and he loved to borrow things and forget to return them. He was a compulsive liar, and he called his mother "Moose Face."

Clearly, if there were a just God, or perhaps even a God at all, what happened to Al and Bob would have been inconceivable. If there were any sense of justice to the cosmos, the stories of Al and Bob would have been far, far different.

Yet the truth can't be denied. Bob died very young, while Al went on to live a long prosperous life.

Things like the story of Al and Bob cause one to question almost everything. How can we believe in a God who apparently allows such things to happen?

What, then, is going on? Do things just happen? Or perhaps God exists, but he allows bad things to happen for his own inscrutable reasons. Or perhaps God exists, but he's not a just God. Or perhaps God exists, but he's not paying attention. Or perhaps God exists, and he's paying attention, and he's all-powerful, but God turns out to be really quirky with a sick sense of humor. I have heard, from reliable sources that MAN is made in God's image. This is not a good sign. How about if God's personality resembles that of those MEN we call the Gambino family?

Maybe the real answer to this line of questioning lies in this concept: things don't *have* to make sense. MAN, the rational animal (from Kenner!) likes to believe that the universe is just as rational as he is. MAN may be seriously screwed up on this one. First of all, just how rational is MAN? After all, MAN is the same "rational animal" who is responsible for the following:

1. World War II
2. The disco era
3. Pepperidge Farm Elf Loaves

Who needs a universe as rational as this guy?

"God is dead," cried Nietzche. "I didn't get a paper today," cried MAN.

MAN has always wanted a God. He *needs* God. For without God, there opens before MAN a void of nothingness, an abyss upon which MAN must struggle to create some vain substitute, some brief intellectual and emotional stay against the black emptiness that stretches, ever widening and yawning, before him.

This is where religion comes in. A MAN is standing there.

Maybe in the desert. Maybe in Atlantic City. At any rate, he's staring right into the abyss and it's staring right back. We're not talking Norman Rockwell here. This is not "MAN stares into the abyss and he's six years old and he's in the doctor's office and he's pulling his pants down and his little butt is just peeping out from the back of his pants and the doctor looks kindly but bald and you can see the little MAN's mother over in the corner looking concerned and worried for her little MAN, but she's also just about to start laughing because she realizes just how fucking charming and cute all this is."

It's not that, buddy. This is the real face-the-infinite-blackness-and-maybe-just maybe-you're-going-to-wind-up-burning-in-hell-or-even-worse-all-those-French-guys-were-right-and-you're-not-even-GOOD-enough-to-burn-in-hell picture.

So let's face the music.

MAN has many religions. Most of them, however, feature another MAN's teachings and/or life. Buddhism is built around that MAN they call Gautama Buddha. Islam is based on the teachings of Muhammad. (Notice that I am not making any glib, wiseass comments about this religion. It's a fabulous religion, and there's no need to do any "follow-up work" on the writer.) Christianity has, of course, Jesus Christ.

Contemporary MAN might, however, want somebody a little more up to date to serve as an avatar for his religion. Today's MAN might want somebody who was at least born in the same century. This might make religion a little more accessible.

For this reason I have decided to start a religion centered around just such an individual. The individual I have in mind *was* born in the same century as you. He is also probably at least vaguely familiar to you.

I want to build a religion around the life and teachings of Frank Sinatra. I've always gotten a great deal of pleasure out of his singing, and I feel that creating a religion in his honor is the least that I could do:

He was with a crowd who had gathered by the lake of Tahoe. In the crowd there were many scribes and pharisees and some people on vacation. Some were with their wives and some were engaged in abominations. Many had paid good money for their abominations.

And he said unto them, "Good evening. SALUT! Welcome to this lovely resort, the home of the beautiful metermaids. Where the elite meet to eat. I want you to always remember, in those immortal words, 'The first shall be last and the last shall be first, but the house is going to do okay.'

"I hope that you're having an enjoyable stay here, and I hope that you remember to love your enemies and be good to those who hate you, especially those who don't drink because when they get up in the morning that's as good as they're going to feel all day.

"I also hope that you've been fortunate. I hope that you're doing better than me and my disciples in that regard. Mr. Martin and Mr. Davis and myself, we ran into a bad streak. Bad streak. Like World War II was a bad streak. Like the bubonic plague."

And he spoke a parable to them. "Can a blind MAN guide a blind man? Will not both fall into a pit? But why dost thou see the speck in thy brother's eye and yet dost not consider the two-by-four in your own eye? Wake up, Charlie. Your train left."

When he had finished all his discourse he sayeth, "In the words of the immortal Joe E. Lewis, you can lead a horse to water, but if you can make him float on his back, then you got something."

Then he began,

The Wrigley Building
Chicago is

The Chicago Cubbies
Chicago is
One town that won't let you down
It's my kind of town
Chicago

Then he went and had a little Jack Daniels. Because, as he had sayeth, last night, he fell off the wagon.

And he returned, full of the Holy Spirit, to Atlantic City. He dwelt there for seven days and nights and he spoke to his followers twice every day, once at nine o'clock and once at eleven.

And he was among a great many followers there and he bid them to sit down and they did as he asked. They were standing and clapping their hands and some of them were calling out to him but he did not acknowledge them but only asked them to sit down. And the people did as he had asked them.

He said unto them, "Thank you. Thank you. Thank you. Thank you."

And he began to talk to them as they sat around him, a multitude of people from all over Judea and the tri-state area. They had come to him to listen to him and be cured of their diseases and do a little gambling.

He lifted up his eyes and he began to speak.

"Blessed are those who know . . . NO CAM-ERAS. No cameras allowed.

"Blessed are those who know what good music is. It's not 'rock.'

"Blessed are those who are always professional in what they do for I will say about them, 'that guy is a pro.'

"Blessed are those who realize that Gary Trudeau is a no talent bum who makes his living by his attempts at humor without regard for fairness or decency.

"Blessed are those who know that Kitty Kelly is nothing but a cheap, lying, no-good broad.

"Blessed are those who are here to share this moment with me. Let's lift a glass and drink to all of us getting along together in this marvelous world. Salut!"

THE TEACHINGS

If any MAN will follow me, let him wear a snap-brim hat and carry a raincoat across his shoulder.

If you be betrayed by your parents and your brethren and your kinsmen and friends, tell them to hit the bricks, Zorro.

As the heart panteth after fountains of water, so my soul panteth. Jilly's. In the wee small hours of.

Why art thou cast down, O my soul? Ring a ding ding.

If you can use some exotic booze, there's a bar in old Bombay.

The End of MAN

ALL MEN MUST DIE. THIS IS NOT SOMETHING I READ ON the ladies' room wall at Bennington; it is, as Sgt. Friday would say, a fact. And it's true for all of us, even Art Linkletter.

I still remember the first time I realized this unfortunate truth (that I would have to die, not Art Linkletter). My first intimation of mortality came to me the evening (it was a Saturday) when my mom and dad took me to the movies.

The feature was something like *Snow White*, but that's not important. It was the little cartoon they showed before *Snow White* that got to me. I'll never forget that little cartoon, even though it couldn't have been more than fifteen minutes long.

Johnny Appleseed. The words still burn in my heart.

For those who have never had the dubious pleasure of seeing *Johnny Appleseed*, let me fill you in. (Have your hankies handy.) Let me preface this by saying that *Johnny Appleseed*, for a ten-year-old boy, is like *Camille* is for you older folks. I feel that I am capable of relating the story of Johnny Appleseed, but only on paper. In person, I'd be sure to become a weeping, quivering mess before I got to the end of the narrative.

Johnny Appleseed is, of course, a cartoon. A Disney cartoon.

That means that the blues are bluer, the reds redder, the yellows yellower. The cartoon runs about fifteen minutes. I'm guessing here because I spent several minutes with my head in my hands, sobbing.

Here's how it goes, told in as controlled a manner as I can manage.

The cartoon begins. We see the sky. It's a very cloudy day, but the clouds are snow-white. The next thing we see is Johnny. He seems to be a teenager. He is asleep, legs on the ground, head leaning against the fence. An older MAN comes up to him. This older MAN seems somewhat dream-like. Since I was a Catholic school kid, I thought that he might be an angel. He wakes up the sleeping Johnny and begins to berate him. The "angel" tells Johnny to stop being lazy, find something to do. Johnny asks him what it is that he should do. The angel gives Johnny his life's work. He tells Johnny to plant apple trees. Johnny is a tad skeptical. He wants to know just where the angel thinks he should plant all these trees. The angel tells him that he should plant apple trees *everywhere*. Johnny says okay. Then he starts.

For the rest of the cartoon we see Johnny busy planting apple trees. He gets so busy at this task—and doing virtually nothing else—that people start calling him "Johnny Appleseed." He becomes very famous. However, he also becomes something else.

Old.

After ten minutes Johnny has gone from a fresh-faced youth to a really old guy with a thick, long, white beard. He starts to develop a little stoop. He starts forgetting things. He no longer thinks about women. He takes frequent naps.

This guy just gets really old. Johnny Appleseed, once not much older than I was, is now an old guy.

So far, things aren't that bad. Even at ten years old, however, I knew what was coming, and I started to dread it.

About fifteen minutes into all this, we see the fruits—if you will—of Johnny's labor. There are apple trees with apples on them everywhere you look. People everywhere are talking about Johnny Appleseed. Johnny Appleseed is a legend. People are writing songs about him. He's as famous as a person can be.

Then, of course, came the ending.

Johnny looks over his life's work and decides that it is good. He's a little tired (he must be about a hundred years old by now), and he decides to take a little nap. He falls asleep. Then came the dreaded music. That music they always play in Disney cartoons: the strings, the choir. I knew what was going to happen. I could feel a little thing in my eyes, some water build-up. Then came the voice over, Tex Ritter, I think.

It went something like this:

So Johnny Appleseed lay down for a long sleep. He had earned it. All around America were the signs of his work, apple trees everywhere you looked. And that day Johnny put down his apple seeds and went to that great apple orchard in the sky. And to this day when the sky is filled with bright white clouds, it's like an orchard in the springtime. Johnny's never really gone. All that you have to do is look up into an early spring sky. There you can see the apple blossoms, and in a way, there you can see Johnny.

Needless to say, at this point I started crying. I didn't start quietly sobbing, though, like a lot of the kids (and some moms) sitting around me. Oh no. I started crying my goddamn head off. I wouldn't stop. There would be no *Snow White* for me. The evening's entertainment was all over.

My parents took me out to the lobby because I was bothering everyone around me. They tried. They hugged me. My mom whispered "nice thoughts" in my ear, but it was impossible. There was no turning back. I had been shattered and there was no putting the pieces back together. My dad grumbled, but they had to take me home and put me in bed. If this had happened today, I'm sure that I would have been heavily sedated.

Maybe I would have wound up hooked up to an IV drip.

The next day, I was fine. Or at least I appeared fine. But, of course, I knew that I would never again be really fine. It wasn't that I had been introduced to Johnny Appleseed. No, it was quite a bit grimmer than that. I had been introduced to somebody who is always walking around out there, but someone that I had, until that evening, failed to notice.

Death. My death.

My next brush with death also took place in a movie theatre. This time it didn't even involve a MAN. What it involved was a dog. This dog's name was, of course, Old Yeller.

You are probably familiar with this classic, but those few who are not, allow me to tell you briefly the saga of Old Yeller. To begin with, Old Yeller's name really isn't Old Yeller. It's "Old Yellow." However, the dog is owned by simple country folk who are hardworking, God-fearing, and don't own a dictionary. Old Yeller is a really good dog. He's smart and loyal and, most important, he's very lovable. He is loved by almost everybody, but he is most loved by a little boy who is about the same age as many of the little boys watching *Old Yeller*. For about ninety minutes, you get really attached to Old Yeller, and you really start to *empathize* with the little boy. Then, without warning, the tone of the movie changes rapidly. Old Yeller, acting in his usual courageous fashion, defends his little boy from an attacking coyote. The coyote gets in a few bites, but Old Yeller wins by a clear-cut technical knock out. All is well. A couple of weeks of rest and Old Yeller will be as good as new. He'll be back to doing his usual thing: helping all humanity in a totally selfless and dedicated fashion. However, there's only one little problem. That coyote had rabies. He bit Old Yeller. Now Old Yeller has rabies. There's only one thing to be done. I'm sorry, little Jimmy (NO! [my reactions in parentheses]). We're going to have to (NO! NO! NO!) shoot Old Yeller (NO! NO! NO! [loud screaming and crying]).

After *Old Yeller* my mom and dad thought that maybe it was a good idea if they stopped taking me to see certain kinds of movies. I went along with this program.

Today, my mom and dad are up there with Johnny Apple-seed. I've gotten pretty used to the idea that someday I'll be joining them. Yesterday afternoon I was watching cartoons with my son Frankie, who is six. They were showing some of the old cartoons. They showed the one about the little frog who sings George M. Cohan songs, but only when nobody can hear him or see him, except for this one little man. They showed the one where Elmer Fudd and Bugs Bunny are in a Wagnerian opera, and Fudd sings his wonderful "Kill the Wab-bit" aria. We are having a great time sitting on the couch. My son seemed to like these old cartoons as much as I do.

Then it happened.

First I heard Tex Ritter's voice. I looked up at the TV and saw. It was a cloudy day. Hundreds of white, fluffy clouds. Yes. It was Appleseed time.

I got up from the sofa.

"Aren't you going to watch this one?" my son asked.

"Already seen it," I said. I went upstairs.

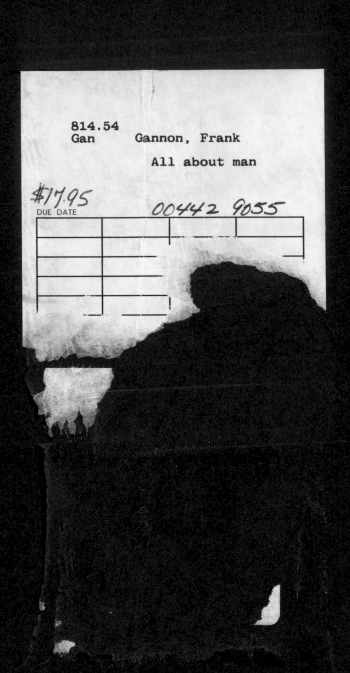